5.00
BT

7202

Date Due

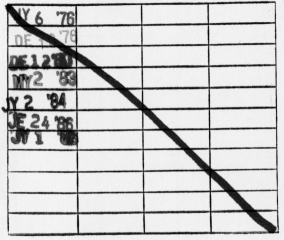

JY 6 '76			
DE 13 '76			
DE 12 '76			
MY 2 '83			
JY 2 '84			
JE 24 '86			
JY 1 '86			

THE POLITICS
OF FEDERAL COURTS

Lower Courts in the United States

THE POLITICS
OF FEDERAL COURTS
Lower Courts in the United States

RICHARD J. RICHARDSON
University of North Carolina

KENNETH N. VINES
State University of New York at Buffalo

 LITTLE, BROWN AND COMPANY
Boston

FIRST PRINTING

*Published simultaneously in Canada
by Little, Brown & Company (Canada) Limited*

PRINTED IN THE UNITED STATES OF AMERICA

To
Matthew and Kenneth
Jon, Anna, and Ellen

PREFACE

Reflecting upon the processes by which this work was produced increases our awareness of the social origins of scholarship, for many individual scholars and institutions have assisted us. Jack Peltason has pointed the way and lent substantial encouragement by his pioneering studies of lower court politics. Herbert Jacob has not only shared his great capacities for friendship and intellectual dialogue with us at numerous times, but has read the entire manuscript with attention both to theory and detail. Glendon Schubert has shared his wit and profound intellectual criticisms with us, helping to put the whole enterprise into proper perspective. Samuel Krislov reacted to our work in valuable ways. But, it is part of the social system of scholarship that authors who have profited so much from others do not also use others to excuse their errors. Finally, we are indebted to the Tulane University Graduate Council of Research, Western Michigan University, the State University of New York, and to Little, Brown and Company for financial support and moral encouragement and Lynne Marcus for her editorial supervision.

RJR
KNV

CONTENTS

THE POLITICS
OF FEDERAL COURTS
Lower Courts in the United States

INTRODUCTION

Politics in the federal courts is usually identified with the one Supreme Court. But the judicial system consists of many courts performing diverse functions in numerous places, resulting in a complex judicial politics. Although the nine Supreme Court justices are most in the public eye and the few decisions they make are accorded widespread attention, several hundred lower court justices also decide many cases affecting a variety of interests and subjects. Measured against the number of decisions made, the size of judicial staff, and the extent of court organization in the lower courts, the Supreme Court and its activities account for but a tiny fraction of the total federal judicial behavior. These considerations suggest that an accurate picture of the American judicial process must reflect the complexity and diversity of the judicial system.

CHAPTER ONE

Like other governmental agencies, the lower federal courts consist of individuals who interact within an institutional framework, making decisions in response to differential pressures and demands. The decisions reflecting these various inputs embody a multiplicity of policies that resolve conflict in society, establish political values, and have varying degrees of impact on other political and social agencies. Lower courts are neither insulated from nor irrelevant to the political and social system. Their activities involve many of the same social issues and clashes of interests that are present in the political system at large. Hence, lower courts are political institutions, suitable for study by the same conceptual and analytical methods found useful in the analysis of other political agencies.

Given the complexity of demands on lower courts, we would

expect an uneven impact from their judicial output. We cannot conclude, however, that lower court decisions are necessarily less important than Supreme Court decisions. This is an empirical question that must be investigated. Although the impact of court decisions will not be considered in this work, we think it important to warn against untested assumptions about the relative significance of courts within the judicial system. It may be that in particular situations and measured by cumulative effects, lower court decisions have greater impact than those of the more publicized Supreme Court. Although the consequences of Supreme Court decision making seem great, we can not assume that lower court decisions are inconsequential without careful investigation.

Problems of Lower Court Analysis

Although political scientists have generally focused their attention upon the Supreme Court, more than a decade ago Jack Peltason called attention to the importance of lower courts. He attributed the imbalance in judicial analysis to the tendency to regard only the justices of the Supreme Court as worthy of study by students of politics. He also observed that the lack of concern with other judges "apparently grows out of the assumption that the Supreme Court justices make policy and other judges perform the routine task of applying it." [1]

Peltason was concerned with the district and appeals courts of the federal system, even though he recognized that there are other lower courts, such as the Court of Claims, the Court of Custom and Patent Appeals, and the Court of Military Appeals. There is considerable justification for focusing upon the district and appeals courts since the core judicial process by which most cases are handled concerns the actions and interactions of these two courts. Lower courts other than the district and appeals courts are "special" courts and deal only with cases in certain restricted areas. The district courts, however, are central to the federal judicial process not only because they are the most numerous and widely distributed

[1] Jack Peltason, *Federal Courts in the Political Process* (Garden City, N.Y.: Doubleday, 1955), p. 13.

courts but also because through them most cases are initiated in the federal system. The appeals courts in the regional circuits, on the other hand, are the primary means by which most appeals are handled. It follows that the actions and interactions of the district courts and regional appeals courts are the central processes of the federal judiciary.

Since Peltason wrote, important advances have been made both in extending the boundaries of judicial theory and in building up a more comprehensive body of knowledge of other courts.[2] There has been progress toward explicit description and conceptualization of the very courts with which Peltason was concerned. Even so, the majority of sophisticated research on the federal courts, on the theory of judicial process, and on the identification of judicial behaviors has continued to concern mainly the Supreme Court.

The relative neglect of lower courts in political science stems from a number of causes, some of them related to the nature of lower courts themselves, others rooted in the development of judicial studies.

The Upper Court Myth: One distraction from the examination of the lower courts was the early tendency on the part of public law scholars to utilize legalistic frames of reference to study judicial institutions. That is, cognitive and evaluative assumptions regarding judicial behavior and judicial institutions were adapted from the legal culture as explanations of how courts and judges actually behave. This orientation discouraged a social science examination of the judiciary; it was especially injurious to the study of lower courts because its assumptions of judicial hierarchy located all power and decision making in the high court.

Lack of Appropriate Models: Although legal theories doubtless were the most important factor inhibiting examination of the lower courts, other elements, intrinsic to the nature of the lower courts

<hr>

[2] For examples see Herbert Jacob, *Justice in America* (Boston: Little, Brown, 1965); Glendon Schubert, *Judicial Policy Making* (Chicago: Scott, Foresman, 1965); Joseph Tanenhaus *et al.,* "The Supreme Court's Certiorari Jurisdiction: Cue Theory," in Glendon Schubert, ed., *Judicial Decision Making* (Glencoe: Free Press, 1962); Sheldon Goldman, "Voting Behavior on the United States Courts of Appeals," LX *American Political Science Review* (1966), pp. 374–383.

limited the amount of investigation. Until Peltason's work, theories of judicial politics usually were applicable only to the Supreme Court and to the particular institutional characteristics of that body.[3] Theories dependent upon the existence of a collegial body of judges, all hearing the same cases, rarely were applicable to institutions presided over by a single judge or by an *ad hoc* committee different for various cases. This meant that theories based upon bloc analysis, scale measurements, or group strategies could rarely be utilized in studies of the district or appeals courts.

Character of Lower Court Data: In its busiest years the United States Supreme Court makes no more than three hundred or so decisions. A number of these decisions are highly visible and are discussed in the mass media. The individual cases are often identified. The decisional output for a year and, more systematically, for several years can be easily handled by judicial scholars, and, consequently, theories of judicial behavior have been based upon these kinds of data. In the lower courts, on the other hand, thousands of decisions are made in a single year in both district and appeals courts. Such a quantity of decisions cannot be readily handled in its entirety as the Supreme Court's data can, and necessitates special methods of data gathering such as sampling. Moreover, lower court decisions often differ in structure from Supreme Court decisions and take a number of forms such as jury trials and pre-trial decisions that are unknown in the Supreme Court. To the student of judicial politics accustomed to the data of the Supreme Court, decisional materials from the lower courts may seem massive and obdurate, presenting difficult problems of analysis.

Relative Lack of Visibility of Lower Court Decisions: Lower court decisions are seldom picked up by the mass media or singled out for individual attention, whereas Supreme Court decisions are frequently presented in a way that stimulates investigation of patterns of policy formation. The low visibility of lower court decisions removes an important stimulation often leading to investigations or curiosity about the decision making process.

---

[3] One major exception is the seminal work of Felix Frankfurter and James M. Landis, *The Business of the Supreme Court: A Study in the Federal Judicial System* (New York: Macmillan, 1927).

Nature of Lower Court Decision Making: A Supreme Court decision often seems to represent the end of the judicial process, furnishing a decided product that is attractive as a subject for analysis. Lower court decisions, on the other hand, appear to represent an initial stage of legal conflict or appeal. The decisions are frequently modified and may represent an indecisive or transitional stage in the judicial process. They require the analysis of relationships with other courts and interactions in the decisional process and are not readily treated according to the static models of the Supreme Court; nor are they, for these reasons, always considered interesting materials for analysis.

The Judicial Subsystem

One special problem in the study of all judicial institutions is the handling of their legal and political aspects. Courts engage in some activities which are usually seen as legal and others which are commonly identified as political. Yet the two concepts are often not clearly differentiated and analyses are ambiguous because no suitable scheme of analysis illuminates both the political and legal features of courts. However, it is quite clear that both legal and political functions are present in courts. In the structuring and shaping of demands, in the language and symbols of court decisions, and in the definition and limitations of policy outputs we may observe the presence of legal values. Moreover, the identity of actors in the judicial process and the names given to many court procedures are legalistic rather than political.

Visible as legal orientations are, of equal significance are democratic influences on the judiciary. Democratic orientations can be seen most frequently as influences characterizing pressures and demands on the courts. In addition, the names given to participants as well as to important activities in the court involve democratic terminology. A useful way of looking at these legal and democratic facets is to regard them as subcultures of the larger American political culture. Both subcultures embody fundamental orientations toward aspects of the judiciary including: (1) cognitive orientations that concern knowledge of the judicial process and provide theories and concepts for intellectual mastery of the objects and processes in judicial institutions; (2) affective orientations that deal with the attitudes and feelings held toward judicial actors, roles, and policies of the federal courts; and (3) evaluative orientations that refer to opinions and judgments concerning estimates of various aspects of the judiciary.

We may observe conflicts between these orientations in certain public controversies concerning aspects of the federal courts. Examples include differences over the appointment of judges, the relative weight to be given to legal and political experiences, or the degree to which the decision making process should be responsive to legal values and democratic values. Because of the important roles of the democratic and legal subcultures in the federal courts, it is desirable to examine in more detail the values, participants, and interests of each.

The Legal Subculture

The legal subculture touches many phases of the judicial function. It includes, for example, rules and norms governing the judicial process, the recruitment of judges, and the behavior of judicial actors. Important examples are the insulated posture that judges are expected to maintain from pressures and interests, the litigation inputs that are admissable for decision making, and the sorts of guidelines judges should use in arriving at decisions. Important features of the legal subculture result from accumulated norms and expectations that are embodied in legal guidelines, precedents, or traditions. Legal values are maintained in the political system through socialization and constitute relatively stable sets of perceptions of the judiciary expressed and institutionalized by legal groups.

Legal orientations do not exist in a vacuum, but are expressed in institutions that articulate values into the political system, perform the tasks of socialization through professional training and associational contacts, and bring pressure to bear upon important questions concerning the courts. Among the groups and institutions that express legal values are the law schools, the bar associations, the judicial councils, and other groups that spring from the institutionalization of the "bench and the bar." Such groups are the primary advocates of legal values. These representatives of the legal subculture, however, do not represent a monolithic front and disagree sometimes on such questions as the manner of legal professional training, how decisions should be made in the courts, and how judicial elites should be selected. Yet, in the main, representatives agree on policy questions involving the judicial process, and they concur on codes of behavior governing the activities of judges, lawyers, and the clientele they serve. They also hold attitudes in common concerning how violations of the codes of behavior should be sanctioned and when and how legal actors should be disciplined for infractions.

The Democratic Subculture

The courts are one of many institutions operating within the American political system that respond in varying ways to democratic values. Throughout American history, the democratization of institutions has progressed. Conflicts over the development of popular responsibility have been major issues in the evolution of the democratic society. The remote and removed institutions, once highly praised by Madison [4] for filtering out the popular passions, have one by one succumbed to the values of an expanded electorate, expressed in the form of popular and representative elites. Of all the federal political institutions, the federal courts appear to have been least affected by democratic revisionism.

Consider explicitly the extent to which the courts have lagged behind the Congress in providing for democratic controls: (1) members of the legislature are elected directly by voters, but federal judges are appointed; (2) members of Congress stand for office at regular intervals and must compete for re-election, but federal judges are appointed for life; (3) judges are shielded from the direct operation of such fundamental democratic forces as political parties, pressure groups, and public opinion that are a fundamental part of congressional politics; (4) judges do not interact regularly

[4] James Madison, *The Federalist, Number X.*

or directly with other political officials, but congressmen do so
with little restraint; and (5) legislators have strong constituency links
and service identifiable clienteles, while judges tend to have weak
constituency ties and shifting clienteles. Given the apparent anti-
democratic character of judicial institutions, it is remarkable that
the lower courts have continued to operate in the American political
system, acutely sensitive as that system is to the values of popular
responsibility.

The courts have survived in democratic society through extensive
linkages with the democratic subculture. In contrast to the clear
influence of the legal subculture over the federal courts, the influence of the democratic subculture is somewhat less visible. However, a close examination reveals that elements of the democratic
subculture are involved in the most important questions concerning
the federal judiciary.

Very often, legal elites such as bar associations and judicial councils are more noticeable spokesmen for the federal judiciary than
are the spokesmen of the democratic subculture. However, representatives of the democratic subculture, such as members of political
parties, members of social and economic groups, and local state
political elites, can also be observed commenting on controversial
questions. In matters like staffing the courts, determining their
structure and organization, and fixing federal jurisdiction, democratic representatives have access through Congress and through
other institutions that are influential in establishing judicial policy.
Although Congress provides a main channel to the federal courts,
access for democratic values is also obtained through the President,
the attorney general, and through nonlegal officials who deal with the
judiciary. In addition, the location of federal courts throughout
the states and regions renders them unusually susceptible to local
and regional democratic forces.

Although direct electoral control, the most visible form of popular
control, is not a feature of the operation of the federal judiciary, other
forms of popular control may be frequently observed in the day-to-
day operation of federal courts. Nonelectoral methods of democratic
involvement may be seen in the influence of political parties, in the
representation of group interests, and in the activity of state and

local elites. These forces may be seen at work in selecting judicial staff, intervening in decision making, and in shaping the organization and the structure of the courts.

The interaction between the two subcultures — legal and democratic — results in a judicial process and structure accommodating to both. The imprint of both subcultures may be frequently found throughout judicial institutions. Consequently, federal courts respond to a variety of influences which results in varied policies reflecting elements of both subcultures, not a monolithic body of judicial output. The conflict between judicial actors, the difference in policies, and the patterns of alliance and support evident in the judicial system are obvious consequences of the influences of both cultures within the courts. Therefore, any conception of lower court politics must take account of legal and democratic subcultures as these affect the entire judiciary.

A Framework of Analysis

Several models present a picture of the federal court system. Among the most useful are those by Glendon Schubert in *Judicial Policy Making* and by Thomas Jahnige and Sheldon Goldman in *The Federal Judicial System*.[5] However, a model that illuminates lower court characteristics and deals explicitly with the legal and democratic features of the judiciary is needed.

We present such a model in Figure 1. It portrays the function of inputs from American society into the federal courts, shows how judicial institutions reflect these demands and in turn transform them into policy, and finally, indicates the impact of divergent policies on the rest of the system. The picture shows how various elements interact as a whole.

Figure 1 suggests that two aspects of the political culture, the democratic and legal subcultures, are especially important in structuring the values and interests that furnish inputs to the political process in relation to the judiciary. We see that while the democratic and

[5] Schubert, *Judicial Policy Making,* p. 106; Thomas Jahnige and Sheldon Goldman, eds., *The Federal Judicial System* (New York: Holt, Rinehart and Winston, 1968), p. 4.

The Judicial System   FIGURE 1

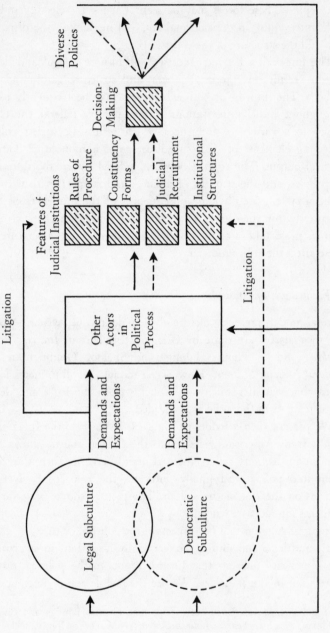

legal subcultures involve quite different aspects, they sometimes exercise overlapping influences. Demands and expectations emerge from the legal and democratic subcultures and interact in the political process, which, in turn, establishes features of judicial institutions. The effects of both subcultures may be observed throughout the judicial system in rules of procedure, constituency forms, judicial recruitment, and institutional structures. Through these judicial institutions additional inputs, placed by litigation, are transformed through decision-making into a manifold of policies flowing from the judicial system.

Based upon the framework suggested by Figure 1, the following chapters deal with significant features of the lower courts. Among these are included some aspects of the demand process, features of the decisional process, indications of policy output, and phases of the interactional process of the judicial system.

We begin our examination with the historical development of the lower federal courts, not only because the evolution of the system presents in sharp detail the conflicts and fusion of the legal and democratic subcultures, but also because the consequences of this long process materially affect the contemporary functioning of the system. Historical decisions determine what demands may be funneled into the system, the forms these demands must take and where they must be placed, and the institutional structure that will receive them. The judicial system built through historic adjustment and modification functions today, and the historic molds have become important political variables in its operation.

In Chapter Three we explore the constituencies in which the lower courts operate. Lower court constituencies place judicial activities in a variety of settings, both regional and local, that not only limit the decisional effects of these activities but also influence the nature of inputs into the courts. Hence, differences among constituencies become important in lower court behavior.

We next turn to judicial recruitment for the lower courts. An examination of formal and informal factors affecting the selection of lower court judges tells us much about the character of actors staffing the courts. It also suggests the variety of experiences and socializing forces that are channeled into the courts by recruitment.

The conflicts over judicial selection are a crucial area in which legal and democratic subcultures interact and one in which important conflicts between interests are especially visible.

We investigate the decisional activities of district courts and courts of appeals in Chapters Five and Six. An exploration of district court decisions provides data on the most common and widely used phase of the federal judicial process. Not only are initial decisions made at the district level, but the shape and structure of appellate litigation is also determined here. Appellate litigation is primarily considered in the regional chambers of the United States Courts of Appeals, where collegial courts review and terminate most appealed findings in the system. Chapter Six explores the process of appeal, politically and structurally different from district court activity.

We next look at the linkages of lower courts to the Supreme Court. Most cases decided in the Supreme Court begin in the lower courts. The few that are reviewed constitute the avenue through which the Supreme Court relates and interacts with the lower courts. Chapter Seven examines the character of the cases reviewed, their disposition by the court, and the interactional patterns between lower courts and the Supreme Court.

We conclude by looking at lower court politics in terms of the model we proposed for examination in this introductory chapter.

THE POLITICS OF
FEDERAL COURT
DEVELOPMENT

Although much less salient than the Supreme Court, the lower federal judiciary has been of continual political importance throughout American history, often creating major controversial issues. Such issues are of more than historical interest, because the present operation of the judicial system is rooted in past development and practices.

The institutional changes in the lower courts have generated frequent conflicts between the aims of the democratic culture and those of legal interests. In addition to the conflict of subcultures, certain differences within the democratic culture have been particularly important in the development of the judiciary, namely, the long, continuing struggle between supporters of states' rights and supporters of nationalist interests. The conflict has been complicated by

CHAPTER TWO

shifting alliances; sometimes legal interests have joined states' rights advocates, and in other instances they have allied with nationalists.

These struggles over court development are not merely issues of the past. The same kinds of conflicts continue today and are related to past conflicts. The proposals for change in judicial organization in the 1960's have called forth such reactions as that of Representative Emanuel Celler when he observed, "They won't have their way as long as I am chairman of the House Committee on Judiciary." [1] The Brooklyn Democrat referred to an attempt by an unidentified "maverick group" in Congress to have the Fifth Judicial Circuit's boundary lines redrawn to include South Carolina and Virginia. Such an action would greatly strengthen conservative

[1] *The New York Times,* July 5, 1964, p. 42.

Southern appellate judges, because it would take them out of a minority position in the Fourth Judicial Circuit and enable them to help create a majority in the Fifth. Although he agreed that the present circuit boundary lines are "geographically absurd and demographically ridiculous," Celler disdained any plan for new boundaries which would enhance the power of conservative forces. Such concern with the politics of structure is solidly in the tradition of the history of lower court institutions.

A historical view of judicial development thus enhances our understanding of the contemporary judicial system. Such a view emphasizes the processes by which the judiciary has developed and shows how diverse interests are accommodated within the judicial structure.[2]

Certain phases of the federal courts' historical development are particularly significant and may be considered especially relevant to the history of judicial institutions. It is principally these historical periods that we discuss in this chapter.[3] The politics of lower federal court development began in the Constitutional Convention.

The Initial Conflicts and Decisions

The provision in the United States Constitution for lower federal courts is deceptively simple. Allowance is made for "such inferior Courts as Congress may from time to time ordain and establish."[4] This phraseology, deliberately adopted by the Constitutional Con-

[2] For an example of the value of historical perspective see Herbert Jacob, "The Courts as Political Agencies — An Historical Analysis," in Kenneth N. Vines and Herbert Jacob, *Studies in Judicial Politics* (New Orleans: Tulane University, 1962), pp. 9–50.

[3] This chapter is especially indebted to four historical works. These are Evan A. Evans, "Fifty Years of the United States Circuit Court of Appeals," IX *Missouri Law Review* (1944), pp. 189–231; Felix Frankfurter and James M. Landis, *The Business of the Supreme Court* (New York: Macmillan, 1927); Charles Warren, *The Supreme Court in United States History,* Vols. I, II, III (Boston: Little, Brown, 1923); Staff of Senate Committee on the Judiciary, 85th Congress, 2nd Session, *Legislative History of the United States Circuit Court of Appeals and the Judges Who Served During the Period 1801 Through March 1958* (Washington: Government Printing Office, 1958).

[4] United States Constitution, Article III, Section 1.

vention, represents a deferred decision, a postponement of the resolution of conflict until the new government was in operation.[5]

The postponement was of short duration, for judicial organization was the first major concern of the new legislators. Senate Bill No. 1, the proposed Judiciary Act of 1789, involved some of the same participants and all the arguments that were involved in the judiciary debates of the convention. Simply stated, the conflict over lower federal courts involved two major questions: (1) should lower federal courts be created at all, or should adjudication of claims of a federal nature be made in the first instance by state courts; and (2) if lower federal courts were created, what limitations should Congress place over their jurisdiction? [6]

Although the Judiciary Act of 1789 provided preliminary answers to these questions, the resolution was not accepted as final by either side in the battle from which it emerged. The conflict continued, and, as participants in the original struggle died, new interests arose

[5] On June 5, 1787, Rutledge of South Carolina suggested, "State tribunals might and ought to be left in all cases to decide in the first instance the right of appeal to the Supreme National Tribunal being sufficient to secure the National rights and uniformity of judgments." To create lower courts would be "an unnecessary encroachment on the jurisdiction of the States and create unnecessary obstacles to their adoption of the new system." He was joined by Sherman and Butler. King, Wilson, and Dickinson joined Madison in arguing that without lower federal courts "dispersed throughout the Republic, with final jurisdiction in many cases, appeals would be multiplied to an oppressive degree," and that to counteract local state prejudices "an effective judiciary establishment . . . was essential." Madison then suggested the compromise that the "National Legislature be empowered to institute inferior tribunals," leaving it to Congress to decide whether and how they should be created. When this motion came up for final vote on July 18, 1781, opposition was expressed by Butler and Martin; Randolph observed that "the courts of the states cannot be trusted with the administration of national laws." The convention adopted Madison's compromise. See Max Farrand, *The Records of the Federal Convention* (New Haven: Yale University Press, 1911), Vol. II, pp. 15, 46; Charles Warren, *The Making of the Constitution* (Boston: Little, Brown, 1929), pp. 326–327.

[6] The "judicial power" of the United States is defined in the Constitution, Article III, Section 2. After much debate, Congress determined that this provision was the maximum range of federal jurisdiction, subject to limitations and restrictions by Congress. The following analysis of the 1789 act is from Charles Warren, "New Light on the History of the Federal Judiciary Act of 1789," XXXVI *Harvard Law Review* (1923).

to champion the old arguments for and against the expansion of the federal judiciary.

To answer the first question — the creation of lower federal courts — the first Congress had to contend with two schools of thought on the federal judiciary. One school, later to be articulated in Antifederalist philosophy, saw the new government as a potential destroyer of the rights of the states. This group wanted federal law to be adjudicated first by state courts and only on appeal by the United States Supreme Court.[7] The other school, represented by Hamilton and Madison, feared that the parochial prejudice of the state courts would deal unjustly with litigants from other states and other countries.[8] Under the leadership of Oliver Ellsworth, later chief justice of the United States, the Senate committee for drafting the proposal of organization set up a judicial system that included lower federal courts. The system was composed of a Supreme Court, consisting of a chief justice and five associate justices; three circuit courts, each composed of two justices of the Supreme Court and a district judge; and thirteen district courts, each presided over by one district judge.[9]

[7] For example, see Tucker's statement in the House debate on August 24, 1789, opposing inferior federal courts and contending that "state courts were fully competent to the purposes for which these courts were to be created and that they would be a burdensome and useless expense"; Livermore's observation that "the State courts have hitherto decided all cases of a national or local import. . . . I think I see a foundation laid for discord, civil wars, and all its concomitants"; Jackson's opposition on August 29, 1789, because the proposed lower courts were too removed from the citizenry and "an offender is dragged from his house, friends, and connections, to a distant spot, where he is deprived of every advantage of former character, of relations and acquaintance." *Debates and Proceedings of the Congress of the United States* (Washington: Gales and Seaton, 1834), pp. 813–834.

[8] The nationalist position was stated by Sedgwick on August 29, 1789, in the House debate: "Suppose a State Government was inimical to the Federal Government, and its judges were attached to the same local policy . . . where would be your redress. Shall we apply to the State Legislatures that patronize them?" Also, Ames on the same day concluded that "they cannot be trusted with the execution of Federal laws. . . . laws dependent on them would throw us back into all the embarrassments that characterized our former situation." Quoted by Warren, "New Light," p. 124.

[9] *Act of September 24, 1789* (1 *Stat.* 73). The original eleven states were each made into a federal judicial district, except Massachusetts and Virginia,

Because the act did create lower federal courts, it has been assumed that the nationalist forces were victorious in their demands. Federal court personnel were separated from the state court systems and somewhat removed from the obstructions of state authority. An equally important political consequence of the act, however, was that the federal court system was not completely removed from state influence. In at least three ways the organization of the federal judiciary was supportive of state interests.

First, the jurisdictions of district and circuit courts were drawn along state boundary lines, with no district crossing more than one state. Thus, from the outset, the federal judiciary was state-contained, with the administrative and political structure of the states becoming the organizational structure of the federal courts. Recognizing belatedly the sectional effects of this structure, Federalists attempted unsuccessfully to change it in 1800.[10]

Second, the federal district judge was a resident of his district. Although appointed by the President, he was declared to be a "superior" officer under the Constitution, subject to approval by the United States Senate. The federal judge was, therefore, a local resident, approved by Senators, adjudicating in his home area, and subject to the continuing influence of his environment.

Finally, the circuit court was organized with a local rather than national focus. The district judges became primarily responsible for preparing the circuit courts' work load, and the Supreme Court justices came into the circuits to hear the cases based on the district judges' advanced work. Therefore, even at the circuit level, the Supreme Court justices came into local areas and participated in cases prepared by local justices. All these features of the lower court system were strongly defended by the antinationalists in 1801 and 1802, so it can be inferred that the organization of the lower federal judiciary in 1789 had appeal for antinationalist interests.[11]

---

which were divided into two districts each. The districts were grouped into three circuits.

[10] See Warren, *The Supreme Court,* Vol. I, p. 186, for bill introduced March 11, 1800 prepared by Hamilton.

[11] In 1802, there was little about the 1789 act that antinationalists did not defend. For a collection of the debates, see *Debates in the Congress of the*

The unique feature of the 1789 act was Section II, the organization of the circuit court, which combined two sets of judges to create
a third level of the judiciary. In defending the organization of the
circuit courts, their architect Oliver Ellsworth observed:

> One Federal Judge, at least, resident in each state appears un-
> avoidable; and without creating any more, or much enhancing
> the expense, there may be Circuit Courts, which would give
> system to the department, uniformity to the proceedings, settle
> many cases in the states that would otherwise go to the Su-
> preme Court, and provide for the higher grade of offences.
> Without this arrangement, there must be many appeals or writs
> of errors from the Supreme Courts of the States, which by plac-
> ing them in a subordinate situation and subjecting their de-
> cisions to frequent reversals, would probably more hurt their
> feelings and their influence than to divide the ground with
> them at first, and leave it optional with the parties entitled to
> Federal jurisdiction, where the causes are of considerable mag-
> nitude, to take their remedy in which line of Courts they
> pleased.[12]

The circuit courts, therefore, were designed to give "system" and
"uniformity" to the "department," and at the same time to perform
this function within the states. A temporary compromise on lower
court organization had been achieved; the Federalists had obtained
lower federal courts, and the antinationalists had placed them within
state containers.

When faced with the question of jurisdiction of the lower courts,
the nationalists felt that the full range of federal jurisdiction granted
by the Constitution should be given to district and circuit courts.[13]

United States on the Bill for Repealing the Law (Albany: Whiting, Leven-
worth and Whiting, 1802), which includes antinationalist John Nicholson's
praise of the 1789 circuit organization suited "for a government like ours,
extending over a large tract of country, and composed of sovereign states,
independent of each other, confederated for purposes of mutual defense,"
February 26–27, 1802, 7th Congress, 1st Session.

[12] Wharton's State Trials, quoted by Warren, "New Light," note 65, p. 77.

[13] In this connection, Representative Smith in his argument in the House
debate that jurisdiction was "too confined" suggested that states need not
fear expanded jurisdiction, for "should the district judge be under any bias,
it is reasonable to suppose it would be rather in favor of his fellow-citizens,
than in favor of foreigners or the United States." August 29, 1789, in Debates

However, to achieve a lower court system at all, the nationalists were forced to modify this demand greatly. The 1789 act gave the lower courts restricted jurisdiction, far less than that permitted by the Constitution.[14] It was not until 1875 that the supporters of the Federalist position were able to extend the full range of federal judicial power to the lower courts.[15]

The Judiciary Act of 1789 has been viewed as a triumph for the Federalist advocacy of a strong national union. However, analysis of the act reveals that it was not a total victory for any interest, but a compromise that pleased few. That Richard Henry Lee, an Antifederalist and strong critic of the Constitution, agreed to report the bill onto the floor of the Senate indicates the degrees to which Antifederalists were successful in their demands. We do not deny that the lower federal judiciary was later to become an instrumentality of Federalist power, but the 1789 act which organized the judiciary and defined its jurisdiction was a disappointment, a partial victory at best, to nationalist leaders.[16]

The Federalist effort to regain the compromised ground lost in 1789 was to be temporarily successful in 1801. The key to the Federalist strategy was the circuit court.

A Temporary Victory: Reorganization
of the Lower Courts in 1801

The federal court system was but a year old when Federalists began their attack on lower court organization. With the support of the Randolph Report, they attacked the organization of the circuit court and urged the elimination of all "circuit riding" by Supreme

---

and Proceedings in the Congress, p. 829. See pp. 825–866 for antinationalist arguments against extension of jurisdiction.

[14] The important comparison between the original draft and the final law was first made by Warren, "New Light," pp. 49–132.

[15] Act of March 3, 1875 (18 Stat. 470). For a brief period in 1801, the circuit courts had full jurisdiction.

[16] See Madison's observation to Pendleton: "The most I hope is that some offensive violations of southern jurisprudence may be corrected, and that the system may speedily undergo a reconsideration under the auspices of the judges who alone will be able, perhaps, to set it to rights," as quoted by Warren, "New Light," p. 130.

Court justices.[17] In 1793, Congress changed the circuit court organization to include only one Supreme Court justice and one district judge but refused to implement the Randolph proposal that separate circuit court judgeships be created to replace the circuit participation by the Supreme Court.[18]

It is interesting that complaints voiced against circuit riding by the Supreme Court justices closely followed the arguments made against the system by Edmund Randolph.[19] Both defended the change as desirable in order to remove the burdensome travel from the Supreme Court justices. But Antifederalist leaders, perhaps remembering Randolph's attack on state courts in the Constitutional Convention, saw in the recommendations an attempt to enlarge the federal judiciary and federal jurisdiction at the expense of their interests. Such a change would lift both the circuit courts and the Supreme Court from the parochial confines of the districts and would separate the upper federal judiciary from state surveillance. Thus, "ardent Federalists with increasing vigor urged Randolph's proposal for separate circuit judges; the emerging Jeffersonian Party came to regard the federal courts as a political adjunct of the hated Federalists." [20]

Climaxing a decade of Federalist effort to implement Randolph's proposals, President Adams recommended in 1799 an "indispensable" revision of the judicial system.[21] Despite Antifederalist opposition, the Act of 1801 was approved.[22] It eliminated circuit riding, created sixteen circuit judgeships, and greatly extended the jurisdic-

---

[17] The report was ordered by the House and was prepared by Edmund Randolph, Washington's attorney general. See *American State Papers, Misc.,* Vol. I, p. 21.

[18] *Act of March 2, 1793* (1 *Stat.* 333).

[19] See Letters from Jay to Washington in *American State Papers, Misc.,* Vol. I, pp. 52, 77, and letter from Jay to King as quoted by Warren, *The Supreme Court,* Vol. I, pp. 89–90.

[20] Frankfurter and Landis, *Business of the Supreme Court,* p. 21.

[21] Message of December 3, 1799, in 10 *Ann. Cong.* 188; for earlier efforts, see 7 *Ann. Cong.* 757, 1116; See a letter of Wolcott to Ames, December 29, 1799, "The steady men in Congress will attempt to extend the judicial department. . . . there is no other way to combat the state opposition," as quoted by Frankfurter and Landis, *Business of the Supreme Court,* note 64, p. 23.

[22] *Act of February 13, 1801* (2 *Stat.* 89).

tion of the lower courts. The "midnight judges" act has generally been viewed as the "dying effort of the Federalists to prolong their domination of government." [23] Recently, however, the suggestion has been made that the primary purpose of the act was not to create new positions for Federalists, but rather to make possible the extension of federal jurisdiction. Pointing out that the Judiciary Act of 1801 was introduced prior to the election of 1800, Kathryn Turner suggests that it was not caused by the election but was rather an integral part of Federalist policy.[24] The act's primary purpose was the extension of federal jurisdiction to suits that could previously be tried only in state courts. Turner observed that Federalists, particularly land speculators and commercial men, wished to enlarge the amount of private civil litigation that could be tried in federal courts rather than in hostile state courts.[25]

Such a view of the act of 1801 does not mean that the Federalists were uninterested in the federal judgeships; they did want to protect the judiciary from Antifederalists. But the act was not a last-minute effort; for ten years Federalists had sought the objectives of the 1801 act. The extension of federal jurisdiction would require additional lower federal courts to assist the Supreme Court with the increased case load. Thus, the circuit courts of appeals became the avenue through which expansion of federal jurisdiction was to be realized.

Following the defeat of the Federalists, the act was repealed.[26] The antinationalists, heaping praise on the old system, restored circuit riding, but did allow the circuit court to be held by a single judge.[27] This slight change proved to be of great importance. Increasingly, the district and circuit court became the responsibility of the district judge alone.[28] Such an arrangement had obvious ad-

[23] Evans, "Fifty Years," p. 194.

[24] Kathryn Turner, "Federalist in Defeat" (Fifty-Seventh Annual Meeting of the Mississippi Valley Historical Association), mimeo. paper, May, 1964.

[25] For other views on the act, see Max Farrand, "The Judiciary Act of 1801," I *American Historical Review* (1900), p. 682.

[26] 2 *Stat*. 132.

[27] 2 *Stat*. 132 (1802); 2 *Stat*. 156 (1802). For Federalist reaction, see Warren, *The Supreme Court*, Vol. I, pp. 206–222.

[28] Frankfurter and Landis, *Business of the Supreme Court*, p. 32.

vantages for those who wished to limit federal jurisdiction and keep adjudication localized. By maintaining the fiction of Supreme Court participation in the circuit court, antinationalists could claim a restoration of the original judicial system. But in practice, both original and appellate jurisdiction was in the hands of the district judge.

The conflicting political interests involved in lower court reorganization in 1801 and 1802 were never more vividly displayed at any time in American history. Reorganization became the key to increased federal jurisdiction and litigation, removed from the parochial confines of the district courts. Without reorganization, the states held substantial power to adjudicate their own conflicts, according to their own standards.

The Final Victory:
The Courts of Appeals

Historians have generally viewed the creation of the courts of appeals as a response to increased federal litigation brought about by the "great increase in population" and the "general business revival which followed the civil war." The strain "imposed severe and increasing burdens on the overtaxed federal Supreme Court." [29] We might assume from this explanation that the courts of appeals appeared on the American scene as a logical, painless, almost automatic response to postwar conditions. Such an assumption is erroneous. The creation of the courts of appeals was one of the most enduring struggles in American political history.

> The reorganization of the judiciary did not involve merely technical questions of judicial organization, nor was it the concern only of lawyers. Beneath the surface of the controversy lay passionate issues of power as between the states and Federal Government. . . . Stubborn political convictions and strong interests were at stake which made the process of accommodation long and precarious.[30]

[29] Ray Forrester, *Cases and Materials of Federal Jurisdiction and Procedure,* Second Edition of Dobie and Ladd (St. Paul, Minnesota: West Publishing Company, 1950), p. 831.
[30] Frankfurter and Landis, *Business of the Supreme Court,* p. 85.

We may ask of the period between 1802 and 1891, why was it so difficult to correct the obviously overburdened judicial system? It was not a question of failure to recognize the problem. For one "brute fact is incontestable: The need for judicial reorganization was recognized by all parties and its fulfillment was indefinitely postponed." [31]

In evaluating this and subsequent periods of judicial history, we must define "judicial relief." In this often-used, innocuous phrase one finds the center of much of the conflict. All parties in the controversy agreed that the federal judiciary needed "relief" and the reorganization schemes that were offered had this objective. But relief may be provided in several ways, some of which would be acceptable to the decision maker and some of which would not.

In any case, a plan of relief acceptable to pronationalist interests could not involve a transfer of power away from the national government to the states. There would have to be some transfer of power, since any plan that took conflicts away from final solution by the Supreme Court would be a transfer of power. But if that transfer were made to the lower federal courts under the supervision of the Supreme Court, then the power of federal jurisdiction would remain intact in the hands of federal agents. It was for this reason that reorganization of the circuit courts continued to be the key to the nationalists' strategy. If the circuit courts could be expanded and given greater control over appeals, then the Supreme Court could be released for policy formulation and adjudication of key cases. The support that the Supreme Court justices gave to the proposals for circuit court reorganization is evidence that they did not view the circuit court expansion as a threat to their power.

The prostate interests, on the other hand, viewed "relief" from a different perspective. They wanted to reduce the burdens of the Supreme Court by reducing its power. Two proposals offered during this period reflect their strategy. In 1826, a proposal was made to reduce federal jurisdiction by transferring powers and cases to the state courts.[32] Additionally, the attempt to repeal Section 25 of the Judiciary Act, which subjected state court decisions to Supreme

---

[31] *Ibid.*, p. 42.
[32] 2 *Congressional Debates*, pp. 547–548.

Court review, was constantly echoed during debates on reorganization of the judiciary.[33] Failing to achieve a reduction in federal court cases and power, prostate interests were willing to accept only minor revisions in the 1789 judicial structure.

Because of the procrastinations of pre-Civil War Congresses, litigation soon outstripped the capacity of the courts. The growth of federal activity, the increase of corporate business, and the expansion of federal jurisdiction by court interpretation all created litigation for a court system ill-equipped to handle it.

The efforts to create an intermediate court of appeals were renewed by Senator Trumbull in 1865.[34] His proposals failed, as had earlier attempts in 1848 and 1854.[35] Unable to win acceptance for an intermediate tribunal, Trumbull proposed the appointment of nine new circuit judges. This measure, approved over much opposition in 1869, also relieved the Supreme Court justices from circuit court duty except for a single term every two years.[36] But the new circuit judges were not able to stop the flood of cases to the Supreme Court, since no new limitations were placed on the right of appeal to the high court.

It is significant that in 1872, three years after the appointment of the nine circuit judges, a Supreme Court justice proposed a new remedy for handling the growing appellate docket. Justice Miller suggested that Congress restrict the right of appeal to the Supreme Court by reducing the high court's review of circuit court decisions.[37] Such a recommendation was unusual, for on the surface the Supreme Court appeared to be requesting the limitation of its own power. But the Miller request, planned for decades by pronationalists, was not a betrayal of Supreme Court power by one of its own

[33] See *Act of September 24, 1789*, Section 25 (1 *Stat.* 73, 85).

[34] 18 *Congressional Globe*, p. 292.

[35] 18 *Congressional Globe*, pp. 398–399; 33 *Congressional Globe*, pp. 924–1210.

[36] *Act of April 10, 1869* (16 *Stat.* 44).

[37] Mr. Justice Miller, "Judicial Reform," 2 *United States Jurist*, p. 1; Miller, "The Law's Delay in the Federal Courts," 5 *Albany Law Journal*, p. 22, as quoted by Frankfurter and Landis, *Business of the Supreme Court*, p. 76.

members. Rather, it was a deliberate effort to shift the burden of
federal litigation to the circuit courts, now enlarged by nine new
justices and safe in the hands of less parochial, federal agents. Congress accepted some of Justice Miller's recommendations in 1875
and began shifting federal business from the Supreme Court to the
circuits.[38]

Pronationalists won in 1875 what they had compromised in 1789,
won in 1801, and lost in 1802. Federal courts were given the full
range of federal jurisdiction, including all cases involving the Constitution, federal law, treaty, and, by removal, cases originally
brought before state courts.[39] The protests against extending jurisdiction reproduced complaints voiced in 1789. They were sum-
marized well in Representative Hoar's position that "I cannot be in
favor of extending all over this country a system which takes from
state tribunals and from state domination what properly belongs to
it." [40] But the times were with the nationalists, who had secured
nine new circuit court judges and some limitation over appeals to
the Supreme Court, and hence the full expansion of jurisdiction
that had been long desired was now possible.

A year after the federal courts were given full powers, George
Washington McCrary, later United States circuit judge, renewed
the Trumbull plan for intermediate appellate tribunals.[41] Congress
delayed. To the complaints that the federal judiciary was breaking
under its new obligations, prostate opponents offered their familiar
remedy, a palliative which they had championed from the outset.
Senator Jonas of Louisiana stated the position of the prostate
opposition:

> The proper course is to go to the root of the evil, and to ascertain
> whether the jurisdiction of the United States courts has been
> providently increased, whether the amendments which have
> been enacted in the last few years, and which have increased
> their business to such enormous proportions, were wisely
> adopted, and whether it is not better for us to go back in our

[38] *Act of February 16, 1875* (18 *Stat.* 315).
[39] *Act of March 3, 1875* (18 *Stat.* 470).
[40] 2 *Congressional Record*, p. 4303.
[41] *Ibid.*, p. 837.

work of legislation and to withdraw a portion of the jurisdiction which has been conferred upon the circuit court.[42]

Although much of the South joined him in the struggle to curtail federal activity, all efforts were futile.

In 1890, the House Committee on the Judiciary reported on a bill introduced by Representative John Rogers.[43] The proposed plan abolished the old circuit court, and in its place created nine intermediate courts of appeal with final decisions in cases arising solely through diversity of citizenship, reserving a right of certification. The new circuit court of appeals was to be staffed by the appointment of two more circuit judges, making a total of three for each circuit.[44] Senator John Evarts of the Senate Judiciary Committee, assisted by a committee of the American Bar Association, changed the proposed reorganization by retaining the old circuit court, but abolishing its appellate jurisdiction. His proposal provided for direct appeal from district and circuit courts to the Supreme Court in certain situations, with most appeals going to the new circuit court of appeals.[45] In a large class of cases, the decisions of a circuit court of appeals would be final, subject to certiorari. The change also provided for the appointment of only one more circuit judge, who, together with the present circuit judge, the district judge, and the Supreme Court justices, could sit upon the circuit court of appeals. Two judges would constitute a quorum. Rogers opposed the Evarts changes, but on September 24, 1890, the bill, with amendments, was approved by the Senate. It was approved on February 28, 1891, by the House, and signed into law on March 3, 1891.[46] The United States Circuit Courts of Appeals were born.

[42] 13 *Congressional Record,* p. 3601, as quoted by Frankfurter and Landis, *Business of the Supreme Court,* p. 84; also see Moulton's statement in the House on June 7, 1884, 15 *Congressional Record,* pp. 286–287.

[43] 21 *Congressional Record,* pp. 3049, 3130.

[44] *Ibid.,* p. 3402.

[45] *Ibid.,* p. 10218.

[46] *Act of March 3, 1891* (26 *Stat.* 826). Notice Mr. Breckinridge's opposition to the proposed circuit court of appeals on February 28, 1891: "I believe that the first and main remedy is the limitation of the jurisdiction to be given to the courts of original jurisdiction, is to take from the Federal judiciary the vast amount of jurisdiction which does not under our system

Creation of the United States Circuit Courts of Appeals freed the Supreme Court, the master of the judicial house, for more important work. Appeals there would be, but not of the routine types. The Supreme Court would hear appeals largely at its pleasure, and would increasingly become an articulator of public policy, with its former work load shifted to trusted lieutenants below.

Postscript to Victory:
1891 to the Present

The federal appellate picture from 1891 to the present has been principally a "mopping-up" operation. Judicial history since the circuit courts of appeals were created has been filled with continued restrictions on the appellate jurisdiction of the Supreme Court and with an enlargement of the personnel and authority of the intermediate appellate authorities. In addition to observing legal restrictions on appeals beyond the circuit courts, the Supreme Court has used its power of certiorari so carefully that it has insulated itself from the bulk of federal litigation.

To observe that there has been a natural extension of the power and responsibility of the appellate courts since 1891 does not mean that such extension has come without opposition. The prostate interests continued to fight the expansion of federal litigation and the appellate court growth.

Certain changes in this period were important. First, the old circuit courts which continued to operate under the 1891 act had to be eliminated. The American Bar Association directed its efforts to eliminating the circuit courts, and in 1897 a special committee of the association was appointed to revise the federal court system in order to consolidate the district and circuit courts, since the circuit courts had no appellate function and often duplicated the functions of the district courts. As the circuit courts of appeals grew, the circuit courts lost their identity and finally, through the efforts of the bar

---

properly belong to it, and turn those cases into the state courts, where they ought to be decided . . . . It is another evidence of the evil of giving an overstimulated patient an additional dose of stimulant," 22 *Congressional Record,* pp. 3586–3587.

in 1911, were abolished and their functions turned over to the district courts.[47]

In addition to abolishing the circuit courts, the 1911 "Judicial Code" was an important step to "revise and codify the laws concerning the jurisdiction and practice of the courts of the United States." [48] It was in this code that "jurisdictional amount" for federal cases was raised and power of both the district courts and circuit courts of appeals expanded.

In 1921, three proposals before the Congress brought legal and prostate interests into conflict. Inspired by Chief Justice Taft and strongly supported by the American Bar Association, the first proposal would have created a core of roving district judges to serve on assignment by the chief justice. The second plan would have permitted the chief justice to assign sitting federal judges to crowded dockets throughout the country, and the final proposal would have created a judicial council in an effort to coordinate the national judicial system.

The "judges-at-large plan" was rejected by the House Judiciary Committee, and prostate interests protested that such a plan would destroy the local ties of district judges and negate the concept of local representation on the federal bench. Although temporary movement of judges from one circuit to another was also viewed as an attack on localism, the chief justice was given this power subject to approval by the senior circuit judges in affected circuits. The efforts of the bar to ensure that judges would administer the courts as proposed in the judicial council plan were viewed by some congressmen as a move to take control of the judiciary away from the legislature. But it too was approved with restrictions, and the judicial council became law in 1922.

A most important modification in the post-1891 period was the "Judges Bill" of 1925, a law which sought to make a complete codification of federal appellate jurisdiction and which set up the basic scheme of organization under which the federal courts now

[47] 36 *Stat.* 1087.
[48] *Ibid.*

operate.[49] The 1925 bill was, like other significant judicial legislation of the period, largely the creation of Chief Justice Taft. He actively sought and obtained support for his proposal from the American Bar Association. By means of a public address before the association in 1922 and frequent communication and contact with major legal figures, he was able to enlist the bar into vigorous activity in support of the bill.

As provided for in the "Judges Bill," the district courts hold exclusive, general, and original jurisdiction. Direct appeal to the Supreme Court was extended only in specified areas. In only one situation may judgments of the circuit courts of appeals be appealed by right to the Supreme Court, and that is when a circuit court has invalidated a state statute. In other cases, appeal may be obtained by certification or certiorari.

The law established ten circuits. Later, the District of Columbia was lifted to full circuit status and the circuit courts of appeals changed to the United States Courts of Appeals.

The purpose of the circuit courts of appeals was achieved as the Supreme Court was relieved of an overburden of cases. Federal jurisdiction was expanded, and appellate activity was shifted from the Supreme Court to the lower courts.

Conclusions

A historical review of lower court development reveals certain important conclusions about its political significance.[50]

Organization of the lower federal judiciary has always been an important political consideration in American history. The original structure of the lower courts in 1789 gave great advantage to pro-state interests. Although created late in American judicial history, the courts of appeals must be seen as part of the political struggle

[49] 43 *Stat.* 936 (1925). See for commentary James Blair, "Federal Appellate Procedure as Affected by the Act of February 13, 1925," 25 *Colorado Law Review* (1925), p. 393; Chief Justice Taft, "The Jurisdiction of the Supreme Court Under the Act of February 13, 1925," 35 *Yale Law Journal* (1935), p. 1.

[50] See conclusions of Evan A. Evans, "Fifty Years of the United States Circuit Courts of Appeals," pp. 230–231.

centering around "inferior court" development which began in the Constitutional Convention. The prolonged delay in their creation was but a reflection of the important changes they would make in the judicial system. For more than a century, their advocates and opponents fought for their interests in judicial reorganization.

With remarkable consistency, pronationalist forces supported revision of the 1789 circuit court plan in order to (1) lift and detach the lower appellate court from the district court and small, sectional districts; (2) use the appellate court increasingly as an articulator of national values and a leveler of judicial sectionalism; (3) make possible the extension of federal jurisdiction to the full limit granted by the Constitution by shifting the burdens of appellate adjudication to the circuits, thus freeing the Supreme Court for a more substantial policy role; and (4) cut back sharply "access by right" to the Supreme Court and permit the Supreme Court to use certiorari as an "access by permission" (after an expansion of jurisdiction in the hands of safe federal agents).

Antinationalists opposed the development of the lower appellate tribunal because (1) it further removed the federal judiciary from the districts and placed individuals before benches which were divorced from "friends, acquaintances, and connections"; (2) they feared it would be a much more attentive and diligent leveler of state interests, more than the Supreme Court had time to be, and much more than was desired; (3) it would permit an extension of federal power and a great increase in federal litigation; and (4) since it would close off appeals at the circuit court level, it would provide a minimum access to the Supreme Court by right.

The conflict between prostate and pronationalist interests was neither simple nor unidimensional. It was made complex by the involvement and shifting patterns of alliance of interests of the legal subculture. While never completely embracing the nationalist positions, organized legal interests did assist the nationalists through their advocacy of intermediate appellate courts, expanded jurisdiction, and the adoption of the judicial code.

The creation of the courts of appeals was a radical modification of the American judiciary. This change eliminated the United States Circuit Courts, permitted a great increase in importance and jurisdiction of both the district and lower appellate courts, and in most cases displaced the Supreme Court as the court of last resort. In over 95 per cent of the cases originating in or removed to the federal courts, the courts of appeals are the courts of last resort.

The political development of the lower courts strongly suggests that the present judicial system is the synthesis of many historical conflicts. To understand the history of this conflict is to better understand the role, processes, and values of the present judicial system.

JUDICIAL CONSTITUENCIES
THE POLITICS OF
STRUCTURE

Constituencies of political officials often mold their behavior in significant ways. Although one usually thinks of constituencies simply in terms of their location and organization, or as a group of people, their political effects are actually far-ranging. They structure the flow of power; they help to define the character of political clienteles; they determine the boundaries of political activities of institutions; and, finally, constituencies influence the patterns of decision making within political institutions.

Although representative functions of courts have rarely been recognized in traditional legal theory, the linkage between political officials and the territory they serve is not just a legislative phenomenon. It follows that a systematic theory of the judiciary must include an examination of the relationship between judicial officials

CHAPTER THREE

and the formal units within which they act. This relationship has been spelled out by an articulate federal judge who observed that "the district judge is personally accountable to the local community and to the local bar"[1] and that the federal judge is tied to the territory in which he performs by a wide range of interactions.

As we have seen the history of lower court organization has largely stemmed from efforts by nationalists and states' rights

[1] Judge John Minor Wisdom, "The Friction making, Exacerbating Political Role of Federal Courts," 21 *Southwestern Law Journal* (1967), pp. 419 ff. For a representational view of the judiciary, see also Carl D. Murray and Malcolm B. Parsons, "Public Attitudes Toward the Representational Role of Legislators and Judges," 9 *Midwest Journal of Political Science* (1965), pp. 167–185.

advocates to organize the federal courts after their own desires. Accordingly, both sides have often been sensitive to the relationship between judicial constituencies and the policies coming from them. Legal groups, on the other hand, although they have given attention to court organization, have primarily been concerned with the physical size and distribution of the federal courts and the courts' adequacy to carry on the business of law.

District Constituencies

In line with informal tradition and by repeatedly affirmed statutory practice, the organization of district courts follows state lines because, historically, federal judicial activities are deeply rooted within the states, which act as basic containers for federal courts. Except for the Supreme Court, whose constituency is the nation, neither the district nor the appeals courts' boundaries violate the wholeness of state territories.[2] A district court may encompass the whole state or a portion of a state, however, because the number of districts in a state varies. Further organizational detail is often added by splitting the districts into smaller units called divisions. Here, again, structure varies among the states, and a district may contain no divisions or it may contain several. As a result, the varying district and division lines make a complex judicial structure characterized by uneven and irregular geographic forms, and suggest, on the surface, a kind of super-gerrymandering practice.

Most federal litigation is heard initially in 88 (in 1965) "district" courts.[3] The districts and divisions are distributed among the states as shown in Table 1. Apart from the consistent structuring along state lines, the organization of district constituencies does not appear to follow any rational plan. District constituency boundaries seem not to be related to any of the factors that normally determine legislative district boundaries, such as size or population. The

[2] The one exception occurs where the state of Wyoming and those portions of Yellowstone National Park situated in Montana and Idaho constitute one judicial district. District boundaries are described in *United States Code,* 28:81–132, 1964.

[3] There are also special courts such as the Court of Claims, which handles limited cases of original jurisdiction.

twenty-five states where judicial affairs are conducted within a single district include such spacious and sparsely populated states as Alaska, Montana, and Colorado, but also include such compact and populous states as Connecticut, Rhode Island, and Massachusetts. Divisions are also inconsistent, for Georgia contains seventeen, Alabama twelve, and Texas twenty-five, whereas New York has four, California five, and New Jersey one. More than half the states have no special divisions, and constituency organization follows district lines.

District and Divisions   TABLE 1

Number of Districts	Number of States
1	25
2	15
3	8
4	2

Number of Divisions	Number of States
Less than 5	37
5–10	9
Over 10	4

District boundaries are very clearly drawn and determine where federal litigation shall take place within the state. On the other hand, divisions are said to be rather "frail" limits on where litigation is conducted within the district.[4] Divisions do determine where particular judges regularly hold court within the district. Because of multi-judge districts, in only about half the instances is there a single judge in a particular district or division [5] and quite clearly the district judiciary does not constitute a single member district system. For that reason, the relation of judge to constituency tends to be more blurred than the relations in many legislative systems where there is one legislator per district. Nonetheless, district judges

[4] Charles Alan Wright, *Federal Courts* (St. Paul: West Publishing Co., 1963), p. 6.

[5] See *United States Code,* 28:133, 1964.

Constituency Characteristics of Selected
District Courts, 1966   TABLE 2

State	Population per District	Number of Judges in State	Population per Judgeship	Number of Divisions	Case Load per Judge
Alabama	N: 1,860,672	6	620,224	12	359
	M: 774,655		516,437		259
	S: 631,413		420,942		313
California	N: 5,586,518	22	620,724	5	322
	S:10,130,686		779,283		346
Connecticut	2,535,234	4	633,808	1	187
Georgia	N: 1,819,920	6	606,640	17	396
	M: 1,281,705		640,852		258
	S: 841,491		841,491		409
Michigan	E: 5,540,674	10	692,584	2	244
	W: 2,282,520		1,141,260		240
Wisconsin	E: 2,421,275	4	807,079	2	152
	W: 1,530,502		1,530,502		233

N—Northern District; S—Southern District; M—Middle District; E—Eastern District; W—Western District.

Sources: *United States Code; United States Census,* 1960; *Annual Report of the Director of the Administrative Office of the United States Courts,* 1966.

are linked to definite territorial divisions within the state for the performance of their judicial functions.

The inconsistencies in structure are examined in more detail in Table 2, which compares the constituency characteristics of six states and lists the district population, number of judgeships, and case loads. It is clear that judicial constituencies differ not only in boundary structure but also in such fundamental features as district population, population per judgeship, and case load per judge. The significance to decision making of variations in judicial constituencies is explored in Chapter Five.

In general institutional terms, the availability of judicial services bears some relationship to the ease with which litigation can be conducted. Moreover, it is hardly arguable that the availability of judicial facilities influences the kind and the amount of court activity as do such factors as differences in the resources, skills, and motivations of potential litigants. For these reasons, we can hypothesize that constituency characteristics do influence access to and use of the courts. This access is now regarded as sufficiently important to be defined as a Fourteenth Amendment right.[6] Inequalities in judicial constituencies, affecting the location and availability of court facilities, are related to decision making and seem similar to inequalities in legislative constituencies.

Appeals Court Constituencies

Most appeals from the district courts are heard in one of eleven appeals courts,[7] one located within each circuit. The appeals courts now have stable constituencies, their own institutional identity, and a separate judiciary; they are no longer the shifting courts with traveling judges of the past.

Table 3 describes the characteristics of the eleven appeals courts. Considered according to geographical patterns, the circuits have a pronounced regional character, following important sectional lines that mark off historical, social, and political differences. Some of the circuits are exclusively regional, such as the First which contains only New England states (except for Puerto Rico), the Fifth (only Southern states except for the Canal Zone), and the Seventh (only Midwestern states). Others are predominantly regional but include one or more outside states, such as the Eighth, which includes six Midwestern states and also a border state (Missouri) and a Southern state (Arkansas).

Comments by Professor Charles Alan Wright, a noted authority on the federal courts, indicate that the regional character of the appeals courts is not only explicitly perceived, but is also valued. Reacting to the 1964 proposal that the Fifth Circuit should be split so that its heavy case load could be eased, he and others opposed the splitting proposal on the grounds that it would reduce the regional character of the courts and make judicial parochialism more likely:

> The great strength of the courts of appeals, since their creation in 1891, has been that they are regional courts, composed of judges who come from a number of different states and have

6 See *NAACP* v. *Button,* 9 L. ed. 2d 405 (1963).

7 Appeals courts boundaries are described in *United States Code,* 28:41–42.

Characteristics of the Appeals
Constituencies, 1966   TABLE 3

Circuit	Population 1960 (in thousands)	Number of Judges	Regional Character	Population per Judge (in thousands)	District Judges per Appeals Judge
First	10,202	3	New England and Puerto Rico	3,401	3.7
Second	21,086	9	Middle (N.Y. and Conn.) and New England (Vt.)	2,343	4.6
Third	18,664	8	Middle Atlantic and Virgin Islands	2,333	4.1
Fourth	17,014	5	Border and South	3,403	4.4
Fifth	29,627	9	Deep South and Canal Zone	3,270	5.0
Sixth	25,155	6	Middle West (Mich. and Ohio) and Border (Tenn. and Ky.)	4,193	5.0
Seventh	19,421	7	Middle West	2,774	3.3
Eighth	15,459	7	Middle West, Border (Mo.), and South (Ark.)	2,208	3.4
Ninth	27,343	9	Pacific Coast and Mountain (Ariz., Mont., and Idaho), Guam, and Hawaii	3,038	4.8
Tenth	8,999	6	Mountain and Middle West	1,500	2.8
District of Columbia	808	9	District of Columbia	90	1.7

Sources: Same as Table 1.

practiced under a variety of systems of law. This has enabled these Federal Courts to avoid the parochialism which too often is the hallmark of state appellate courts, where all the judges are versed in a single system.[8]

It is also clear from Table 3 that the appeals courts in the different circuits vary as to size, number of judges, population, and district

[8] Letter to the editor, *The New York Times,* July 10, 1964.

judges per appeals judge. (The population of the District of Columbia is irrelevant to the size of that court, since the court gets its appellate business from government institutions situated there.) Although there are undoubtedly differences in litigation potential for different populations, there is no indication that the circuit courts are arranged according to such factors. A clear indication is the small population size of the Tenth Circuit which contains few highly urban and industrialized sections, populations generally associated with high litigation potential.

Particularly important is the variation in the circuits' potential to handle appeals. We have measured appellate facilities by noting the ratio of appeals judges to district judges in the circuit. This measure is not perfect, however, since it includes neither appeals from the independent regulatory commissions or government boards nor possible differences among the circuits' potential for litigation. The number of district judges per appellate judge ranges from a low of 1.7 in the District of Columbia and 2.8 in the Tenth Circuit to a high of 5.0 in the Fifth and Sixth Circuits. Although the excellent appellate facilities of the District of Columbia can be justified by the great amount of government business, there seems to be no reason why the Tenth should have relatively more appeals judges than the other circuits.

Variation in the availability of facilities probably makes a difference in the judicial process, since here, as in other political institutions, the character of facilities either encourages or impedes their use by their clienteles.

Malapportionment in the Courts?

We have suggested that differences in constituency characteristics in both districts and appeals courts lead to institutional differences and may affect the adequacy of judicial facilities. Legal studies of court administration frequently discuss such problems in terms of "delay in the courts" and "overloaded dockets" but usually view the problems as a mechanical aspect of the judicial process rather than as a political problem.

Traditionally, malapportionment is not a concept used to describe judicial institutions, although the problems of access and representation, both features of malapportionment, are relevant to judicial problems. In legislatures and courts alike, clienteles seek access to the courts for the purpose of making claims and demands upon the political system and both institutions are located in districts, states, and regions for the convenience of their clienteles. Policy statements by the courts themselves recognize the representational function of judicial institutions.[9] It may be assumed that courts are part of the on-going political process of the constituency in which they are located and function as part of the representational system. One can argue. therefore, that any inequality or inadequacy in judicial facilities violates fundamental democratic values.

This "equal protection" view of judicial constituencies, analogizing them to legislative districts has been given substantial attention in a recent comprehensive work on the reapportionment problem. Moreover, a scattering of suits has been brought in state courts to compel reapportionment of state electoral districts; the United States Supreme Court has called attention to reapportionment in comments from the bench; and there is growing awareness of the significance of the relationship of populations to their judicial constituencies. While the issue of judicial representation in the federal courts has not been accorded the same attention given the state courts, Dixon argues that the "equal protection" argument goes beyond voting situations and applies equally to a system in which judges are appointed. It follows that the problem of democratic equality in institutions of government may clearly be held applicable to judicial constituencies of the federal court system.[10]

Given the fundamental role of court constituencies in the judicial process, there is considerable justification for thinking of a "judicial malapportionment." Certainly the adequacy of judicial staff helps

[9] See Kenneth M. Dolbeare, "The Federal District Courts and Urban Public Policy: An Exploratory Study," in Joel Grossman and Joseph Tanenhaus, eds., *Frontiers of Judicial Research* (New York: John Wiley and Sons, 1969).

[10] Robert G. Dixon, Jr., *Democratic Representation* (New York: Oxford University Press, 1968), pp. 559–564.

determine both accessibility to and effectiveness of courts, and inequalities in judicial staff may affect the expectations of litigants as well as create unfavorable environments for the presentation of policy demands. For these reasons, figures on case litigation are not an entirely satisfactory measure of institutional adequacy. The number of judges available for actions, it can be argued, might well create conditions favorable for litigation and increase it substantially. A constituency deprived of institutional representation in the judiciary may suffer some of the same ills as similarly situated constituencies in legislative malapportionment.

Constituency Social and Economic Differences

Irregularities in districting of federal district courts have resulted in some important social and political differences. Since the districts always follow state boundaries, judicial constituencies usually reflect the distinctive characteristics of state political and social systems. Thus, for example, the two districts in Mississippi take on many of the characteristics of that state simply by being within the state, staffed by local court personnel, serving a state clientele, and handling controversies that grow out of the political and social milieu.

Until recently, federal district courts in the South segregated Negroes and whites in the courtroom, even when litigation was over civil rights and was carried on by Negroes. Southern federal courts have also followed regional custom by not employing Negroes except in custodial and service jobs. As a consequence, the federal courts in the South have been called "frankly white dominated institutions" by the Southern Regional Council. In a recent study of Negro employment in Southern federal courts, the council found that of 1,224 positions only 14 (1.14 per cent) were held by Negroes. Non-custodial and non-service positions held by Negroes consisted of nine deputy United States marshals and five assistant United States attorneys, but no jobs were held in the categories of referee in bankruptcy, United States commissioner, United States clerk, deputy United States clerk, or jury commissioner. One official in Alabama observed, "If it were not for the lone Negro deputy marshal, the District Court in Birmingham would look like the County Courthouse." [11]

Racial segregation in the administration of the courts raises interesting questions about the policy making process. What practical effects do conditions in the courts have on the settlement of issues that themselves involve civil rights? Does the due process conception of "peer equals" have relevance to the way in which courts are administered? Few social scientists would maintain that the decision making process is indifferent to the context in which it is formulated.

Many important local differences among the district judiciaries may be observed within states. Districts sometimes capture sectional features of the state, and these differences are significant because they influence the character of the district court process. Policies are formulated by judges with strong local connections, are administered by a locally appointed and sanctioned court staff, and serve a clientele usually drawn from the district. Juries, selected according to district rules, reflect the social character of the particular district.[12] The rules of federal jurisdiction and the determination of venue assure that cases arising within a district are heard in the court of that district, except rarely when the operation of the diversity clause of federal jurisdiction brings a case from outside the district.[13] Another rule tying the court to its district is the requirement that judges must, except in a few instances, live within the district they serve.[14]

Table 4 illustrates how districts capture important social and economic differences. Judging from the manner in which districts are created, we see no deliberate effort to capture certain populations. The differences result rather from the drawing of district lines along sectional contours. An excellent example of this is the divi-

[11] *Racial Discrimination in the Southern Federal Courts* (Atlanta: Southern Regional Council, 1965). Both quotations are from this monograph.
[12] Fannie J. Klein, *Survey of the U.S. District Court Western District of Pennsylvania* (Washington: Administrative Office of United States Courts, 1960), pp. 30–36.
[13] Wright, *Federal Courts,* chaps. 4–7.
[14] *United States Code,* 28:134, 1964.

sions of the Tennessee districts. There, the low Negro population of eastern Tennessee is reflected in the eastern and middle districts, and the western district mirrors the much larger Negro population of the western part of the state bordering on Mississippi. In similar fashion, sectional Negro-white population differences are followed in the districts of Alabama, Georgia, Texas, Arkansas, North Carolina, and Virginia. Closer examination of the districts reveals other differences as well. For example, some districts contain cities and others have a predominantly rural population. There are also differences among labor union populations, income and occupational groups, and socio-economic features. Although constituency differences are grosser than they are among most legislative districts because of greater size of judicial districts, variations are still distinct enough to merit attention.

Negro-White Population Differences among Judicial Districts in the South TABLE 4

Per cent Negro Population	Districts in South
0– 9	middle Tennessee, eastern Tennessee, western North Carolina, western Texas, northern Texas
10–19	western Arkansas, northern Georgia, eastern Texas, western Virginia, northern Alabama
20–29	southern Florida, northern Florida, middle North Carolina, eastern Arkansas, western Tennessee, eastern Texas
30–39	western South Carolina, western Louisiana, eastern Louisiana, southern Georgia
40–49	middle Alabama, eastern North Carolina, southern Mississippi, northern Mississippi, eastern Virginia, middle Georgia
Over 50	southern Alabama, eastern South Carolina

The impact of district social differences on judicial decision making can be seen clearly in civil rights litigation in the South. Civil rights litigants, the Justice Department, and the appeals courts have all encountered hostility in the district courts of the deep

South.[15] In a direct commentary on the hostile environment of
Southern district courts, some congressmen advocated that the District of Columbia court, rather than local Southern district courts,
be given powers under the 1965 Civil Rights Act to enforce voting
rights. Indeed, the act as passed gives the District of Columbia
court some special powers of enforcement not given to the district
courts.[16]

The Politics of Constituency Development

As Frankfurter and Landis have noted, the two great principles
that have formed federal court organization are the need to accommodate the federal system and the necessity of dealing with a geographically large political system. Although these principles may help
to explain the state and regional characteristics of constituency structure, they do not account for the apparent inconsistencies in organization and staffing. A third rationale should be added, namely,
the immersion of judicial administration in the patronage politics
of the presidential-senate party. Decisions on court organization,
constituency structure, and judicial staff are made by the Senate
in collaboration with the President and sometimes the House
Committee on Judiciary.

Both the size of the judiciary and the manner in which it is distributed are matters of congressional enactment, legislated with the
strong assistance of the President and often on the advice of the
Judicial Conference. Ever since the Judiciary Act of 1789 created
the first body of federal judges and provided for their allocation, the
federal judiciary has been provided for by single legislative acts
which have added to the existing organization incrementally.[17] In
this way the basic pattern of judicial selection and allocation has not
been seriously altered. The staffing policies of the courts conse-

[15] For authoritative description of this and other civil rights litigation in
the Southern federal courts, see Jack W. Peltason, *Fifty-Eight Lonely Men*
(New York: Harcourt, Brace and World, 1961).

[16] *United States Statutes at Large, 89th Congress,* First Session, August 6,
1965, Vol. 79, pp. 437–446.

[17] A listing of the various acts allocating judicial positions may be found
in successive editions of the *United States Code.*

quently resemble those of other organizations in which the entire structure is not rationally reorganized, but altered as politically expedient.

Allocations of judicial positions have been of two sorts: increments of one or two judges at a time, and major increases by the so-called omnibus judges bills reflecting the major tides of the partisan system as administrations change in Washington. For example, the omnibus bill of 1949 provided for twenty-one additional judges, the 1954 omnibus bill called for twenty-three, one passed in 1961 called for sixty-four and one in 1966 called for seventy judges. Each bill followed the important presidential victories of 1948, 1952, and 1960 and was intended to provide patronage for the administration, the Senate, and the state parties. In fact, the omnibus bills represent accumulations of judicial needs and judicial appointments saved for the periods following the national campaigns, when the need for party allocations of important positions is greatest.[18] If there were a central direction of the judicial system, the omnibus bills could be explained in terms of the need for centralized planning and coordination. Such centralized direction for judicial staffing does not exist, however, and the omnibus collections are derived from many individual allocations processed over a period of years by the Senate Judiciary Committee.

A minority of new judgeships results from Judicial Conference recommendation and consequent legislation by Congress. For example, the number of judges for Illinois was increased from six to eight in 1950 and from one to two for South Dakota in 1957.[19] In the main, however, additions to the judicial staff are saved for the large patronage pools represented by the omnibus judges' bills.

The needs for increased judicial staff have thus been satisfied piecemeal by legislation geared to the politics of patronage. Moreover, the process by which the demands for more judges have been made, heard, and legislated has followed a ritual that has now become traditional and may be observed in many volumes of hearings by the Senate Judiciary Committee. Leading advocates of additional judgeships for states and districts are the state's Senators and Repre-

[18] See acts allocating positions in *United States Code.*
[19] *United States Code,* 28:133, 1964.

sentatives who testify in favor of new judges. They are supported by state and local bar associations who appear for testimony or write the committee about the personnel needs of the state. Most arguments for increased judiciary are put in terms of docket congestion, overloading of existing judges, and delay in processing cases in the courts.[20]

Supporting arguments for increasing the judiciary are an ambiguous part of the testimony, relying as they do on statistics on case loads and disposition of cases. In a typical hearing before the Senate Committee, massive statistics are submitted to show that the dockets of the state or district are overloaded and that delay and congestion result. Since delay and congestion are the legal symbols by which the work of the courts is most frequently measured, such arguments and demonstrations are the accepted rhetoric of the committee proceedings.

Only occasionally have attempts been made to change the district structure of a state. Such an attempt occurred in the late 1950's, when the San Diego area of California lobbied for a new district to serve that area.[21] Appearing before the Senate Judiciary Committee was a cluster of San Diego interests, including bar associations, the Oakland Chamber of Commerce, and newspaper representatives. They argued that the new district was needed to accommodate rapidly growing industry and commerce, and that San Diego was entitled to the court as a government installation. The chief judge of the Ninth Circuit and the Judicial Council opposed the new district, however, and the proposal failed in Congress, although the Judiciary Committee reported it favorably.

Unfortunately, arguments over case loads and congestion are based upon notoriously unreliable data. Indeed, accurate judicial data on the federal courts were totally lacking until 1875, and since then have been gathered by the administrative office of the United States courts depending upon the local cooperation of the separate

[20] See *Creation of Certain United States Judgeships,* Hearing Before a Subcommittee of the Committee on the Judiciary, United States Senate, 84th Congress, 2nd Session, June 19, 1956.

[21] *Senate Report,* No. 1158, 85th Congress, 1st Session, August 29, 1957. Ten years later, pressures resulted in the addition of two new districts for California, the eastern and central districts.

courts. There are two difficulties with the present system of statistical analysis. First, the source consists of the work of the administrative personnel in individual districts, who gather statistics in irregular fashion without supervision from a single authority.[22] In addition, the data reveal general patterns of judicial business only, analyzed in aggregate fashion. Useful analysis of variations among judges and districts, according to significant categories and directed by a central administrative authority, is lacking.

Moreover, the figures on judicial business can be and are regularly manipulated for political purposes during hearings on legislation to add new judges. Experienced jurists have sometimes seriously questioned the available figures for case load and delay. Chief Justice Taft, testifying before a congressional committee, called the figures "quite misleading," and referred to the "stuffing of dockets." [23] In contemporary testimony before a congressional committee, it was stated that the number of cases pending tells us very little, for there may be cases that have been on the dockets for a long time. More recently, Chief Judge Charles E. Clark of the Second Circuit, to show that the law's delay is sometimes exaggerated, described ways in which the appearances of delay and congestion may be deceptive and not indicative of the business of the court.[24]

In contrast to the ever-expanding number of positions in the federal judiciary, the number and allocation of districts have remained stable. (Rare exceptions to this were the creation of a third district for Florida in the 1950's and two for California in the late 1960's.) The states are usually divided into judicial districts at the time of their admission into the union, and the districts remain the same even though the judicial staff multiplies. Districts fixed upon admission of the state to the union become stabilized by tradition and are rarely rearranged.[25]

[22] Interview with administrator of the United States Courts, September, 1965.

[23] William H. Taft, "The Attacks on the Courts and Legal Procedure," 5 *Kentucky Law Journal* (1916), pp. 3–24.

[24] Letter to the editor, *The New York Times,* March 12, 1963. Cited in Senate Judiciary Committee Hearings (see note 16).

[25] This conclusion is gained from examination of past *United States Codes.*

The relatively low visibility of judicial constituencies in the political system offers partial explanation for the continued irregularity of structure and the lack of concern for existing inequalities. Only the number of positions within districts and circuits occasions concern and political activity. There in no procedure for modifying judicial districts according to population. The most frequently voiced worry revealed in Senate Judiciary Committee hearings is over convenience for lawyers and other participants in litigation. Inconveniences that arise from distance are easily remedied by legislation requiring the courts to hold session at more places, and these provisions are made without changing basic constituency structures. The organization, distribution, and location of districts and circuits are rarely discussed.

The character of court administration also has strong effect on judicial constituencies since no central direction exists to instill order and regularity in federal court structures. As we have suggested, the judiciary is linked to variable local and partisan values that encourage haphazard administration. The consequences of such a system, with strong roots in localism and individual court independence, have been a lack of central development and orderly planning in the growth and development of the court organization.

The lack of administrative direction in American court organization contrasts with the English system, in which the Lord Chancellor, since the Judicature Act of 1873, has exercised substantial central direction and responsibility for the judicial system. Around the beginning of the twentieth century, there was a movement in that direction by prominent American jurists who were stimulated by Pound's famous address before the American Bar Association and by the writings of Cardozo and Taft. Cardozo advocated the establishment of a ministry of justice that would exercise central direction over the court system, but he stated his ideas mainly in terms of reforming the existing structure.[26]

Backed by the great prestige and activity of Taft, the proposals for reform culminated in the Judiciary Act of 1922, which provided

[26] Benjamin Cardozo, "A Ministry of Justice," 25 *Harvard Law Review* (1921), pp. 113–136.

for a conference of senior circuit judges. The Judicial Conference has two duties with respect to the administration of the judicial system: (1) the recommendation to Congress of legislation relating to the judiciary, and (2) the promotion of effective administration in the lower courts of the federal system.[27] In addition to making recommendations to Congress and the lower courts, the conference assigns judges from one circuit to another, under closely specified conditions.

Although the recommendations of the conference undoubtedly have prestige in Congress, they have not replaced the patronage system in the allocation of judges and are, rather, only one more feature of judicial staffing. The recommendations of the conference have likewise done little to correct the inconsistencies in judicial organization, either in rationalizing its organization or in suggesting more central administration of the system. The independence of the individual courts and their irregularities of organization and structure remain unchanged. In fact, the Judicial Conference is reluctant to make suggestions for constituency changes and has often recommended against such proposals.

The economic and social differences maintained in the vast irregularities and inconsistencies of the federal judicial constituency structure pose a question of fundamental importance: How can a uniform body of national law emerge from such a constituency structure? Certain aspects of this problem are examined in subsequent chapters. Some features of the legal culture have brought a degree of national uniformity and consistency to the court system. This has been accomplished through the socialization of judges, by supervisory controls in the judicial process, and to some extent in the Judicial Conference.

Inevitably tensions have existed between legal and democratic norms, particularly when controversial issues have been involved in litigation. The most visible tension has occurred in Southern judges' handling of race relations. When district judges have been responsive to Southern racial values, conflicts with such agencies as

[27] The Judicial Council's duties are described in *Field Study of the Operations of United States Courts,* Report to Senate Appropriations Committee, April, 1959.

the appellate courts and the Justice Department have occurred. On other occasions, issues such as labor relations have also come into public view. It is clear that the basic nature of judicial constituencies makes for continuing conflict in the judicial process, as "federal judges . . . perform firmly and fully their friction-making, exacerbating political role." [28]

[28] Judge John Minor Wisdom, "Friction-making, Exacerbating Political Role of Federal Courts," p. 428.

JUDICIAL SELECTION
IN THE LOWER COURTS

The recruitment of the federal judiciary is a major method by which political values and behaviors are controlled and predicted in federal courts. Controversies over methods of selecting the judiciary and arguments over the choice of particular judges indicate concern for their orientations. Although recruitment is important for all political institutions, it is especially important in the judiciary because of the quasi-insulated character of courts. Once judges are selected they tend to be shielded from political pressures, except for those pressures that are admissible under the severely controlled channels of the legal process.

For these reasons, recruitment in the lower federal courts has produced intense and visible conflict between the legal and demo-

CHAPTER FOUR

cratic cultures and is a subject of great dispute in federal court politics. Superficially, the influence of both cultures may seem equal in the selection process. The process provides lifetime appointment, which is agreeable to the legalists, but it also brings in the democrats by requiring the advice and consent of the Senate for all appointments. "Blue slips" are sent to Senators at the time of appointment, and telegrams are also sent to the American Bar Association and the state and local bar associations where the vacancy exists. In a similar parallel, the law training that most nominees possess is supplemented by political training and experience. Closer examination of the recruitment process, however, reveals great differences in the influence of the two cultures.

The Selection Process

Since the creation of the lower federal courts, the formal selection process has never been changed. In form, the appointment of federal judges could hardly be simpler: they are nominated by the President and affirmed by a majority vote of the Senate. With the development of congressional committees, approval by the Senate Judiciary Committee has become a kind of semiformal aspect of all appointments.

The most important development in the selection process has been the increase in the number of participants. Through the years, judicial selection in the lower courts has become diffused among a number of individuals and groups. The growth in complexity has not caused any change in formal methods, however, nor has it meant a shift in the locus of appointment power to the new participants. In the following pages we shall consider the sanctioning power of participants in the recruitment process to see whether their roles are ritualistic rather than decisive.

Table 1 describes the diffuse character of judicial recruitment by pointing out the different participants in the initiating, screening, and affirming stages. This selection model implies that there are many paths to the lower federal courts, and that no single sequence

The General Selection Process
for District Courts   TABLE 1

Initiation May Be By: (singly or in combination)	Screening By: (usually all)	Affirmed By: (both)
Senator(s) of presidential party	Senator(s) of presidential party	Senate Judiciary Committee
President or his advisor	President	Senate vote of majority
Local party	Justice Department	
Candidate himself	FBI investigation	
Influential judge	Committee on the Federal Judiciary of ABA	
	Interest groups (usually bar groups)	

of events or group of participants will necessarily be involved in a particular appointment. Indeed, there are variations from state to state, from one national administration to another, from one time to another. The perceptions that participants hold of the appointment process also differ widely.

The present process has developed incrementally. Most important, individual Senators were not present in the initiation and screening of appointments until 1840, and before that time, all congressmen from the state where the appointment was to be made participated approximately equally. Shortly after 1840, the role of the President was modified, because he delegated to the attorney general the formal authority to make recommendations for nominations. Previously, the secretary of state had handled nominations for the judiciary as well as for other offices in the national government. After World War I, FBI reports were initiated as a clearance device for potential nominees, and in 1946 the American Bar Association, through its Committee on the Federal Judiciary, intervened in the process of selection.[1]

Considered in its entirety, however, judicial recruitment is more stable and predictable than its diffuse character indicates at first. Regular procedures have developed in the appointment process, which, with the formal requirements, set standards for the recruitment. By examining and comparing both the controversial, complicated appointments and the seemingly routine appointments, we can abstract a core model which describes the essential features of the selection process. Table 2 presents such a model. The core model narrows the selection process to a few participants; although other participants may set limits, they do not negate the basic procedure.

Historians of judicial recruitment agree that the writers of constitutional provisions intended to place the initiative for making appointments in the hands of the President and to give the Senate a negative check through its power to advise and consent in order to guard against the exceptionally bad appointments that a President

---

[1] Joseph P. Harris, *The Advice and Consent of the Senate* (Berkeley: University of California Press, 1955), pp. 314 ff.

Core Process for Judicial Selection
in District Courts   TABLE 2

Senator(s) of presidential party, and/or local presidential party and president and his advisors	interact to produce a nominee who is then affirmed by	the acquiescence of Senate Judiciary Committee and majority of Senate

might make.[2] Table 2 shows the reversal of roles, in particular the dominance of the Senate. This body began in an auxiliary role but, according to one critic of the selection process,

> has appropriated the President's power of nomination so far as it concerns appointments of interest to senators of the party in power; and the President has virtually surrendered his power directly to local party politics as to appointments in states where senators are of the opposition.[3]

Since the Constitution does not specify how the President is to make judicial nominations, he can use a Missouri plan type of council, consult sitting judges, or use any member of the cabinet for the function. (He used the secretary of state early in the nineteenth century.) In theory, the President utilizes the attorney general, who recommends to the President in a formal letter that a nomination be made. In actuality, the work of preparing the background information and materials that accompany the recommendation has been delegated to the deputy attorney general and his staff. In this way, the preparation of certain basic materials on the nomination has become a part of regular staff work. And although the President does control nominations, as we shall see later, the predominant initiative has passed to the Senate, despite Alexander Hamilton's confident statement that "there will be, of course, no exertion of choice on the part of the Senate." [4]

Two features of American politics have led to the crucial power

[2] For a summary of the evidence see Joel Grossman, *Lawyers and Judges* (New York: John Wiley and Sons, 1965), pp. 24 ff.

[3] Evan Haynes, *Selection and Tenure of Judges* (Newark: National Conference of Judicial Councils, 1944), p. 23.

[4] Quoted in Grossman, *Lawyers and Judges,* p. 26.

which Senators and local parties from the state of the vacancy have. Most important is the historic involvement of state and local influence in the formation of judicial organization, creating the likelihood that Senators would be linked to the courts through their own involvement in state politics. The explicit involvement of Senators in federal appointments in the states has resulted from senatorial courtesy and the part that patronage plays in the support of political parties. Second, since state organizations are important in national party politics, we would expect the power for recommending judicial appointments to lie with state political organizations. Federal judgeships, with their high prestige, life tenures, and relatively high salaries, are the most desirable political appointments that can be made from the states and for this reason are politically important to the Senator and his supporting party organization.

The control that Senators exercise is perhaps best symbolized by the "blue slip" device. As standard procedure, the Senate Judiciary Committee sends to the Senators of the state where the vacancy exists a request to approve or disapprove the nomination that is being considered by the committee. The request is printed on a standard blue form (hence its name). If the blue slip is not returned to the committee in one week, the committee assumes that no objection is raised. It should be added that although blue slips are sent to both Senators from the state concerned, much more serious attention is paid to the opinions of the Senators of the President's party, and comparatively little heed is given to the Senators who belong to the opposition party. The blue slip reads as follows:

> Dear Senator:
>
> Will you kindly give me, for use of the Committee, your opinion and information concerning the nomination of (name, district, name of former judge.)
>
> Under a rule of the Committee, unless a reply is received from you within a week from this date, it will be assumed that you have no objection to this nomination.
>
> > Respectfully,
> > (Signature)
> > Chairman

Examples of the use of the blue slip to voice objections are illustrated by the comments of Iowa Senators Gillette, a Democrat, and Hickenlooper, a Republican, in response to President Truman's nomination of Carrol O. Switzer in the spring of 1950. The blue slip returned from Senator Gillette read as follows:

> I am opposed to the confirmation of Mr. Switzer for this appointment for the reasons which I advanced to his former appointment.
>
> 1. I do not believe him to possess the experience and qualifications necessary;
> 2. There is strong evidence of the nomination being the result of political trafficking;
> 3. The nomination was in negation of senatorial prerogative under the Constitution.
>
> S. M. Gillette

The blue slip from Senator Hickenlooper read as follows:

> I am opposed to this appointment for reasons already recorded with the Committee and stand ready to present my views to the Committee at its convenience.
>
> Hickenlooper

President Truman's controversy with the Iowa Senators, especially Gillette of his own party, was only one of several between the President and the Senators over judicial appointments. (Another was a notable argument with Illinois' Senator Douglas over appointments from that state.) All of these arguments were caused by Truman's failure to consult Senators from his own party about vacancies from their own states, and in no instance did he succeed in getting approval for a judicial appointment that had not received the endorsement of Democratic Senators from the state of the vacancy.

When the President and relevant Senators agree on a nominee for the lower courts, the nomination usually goes through without delay or obstruction. An index to the effectiveness of the core process in securing nominations is the fact that the Senate has rejected less than 1 per cent of the candidates nominated by the President and Senators or local party combination. In such cases the appointment process is routine, and little special notice is taken of the appointment in the abbreviated and perfunctory hearings conducted by the Senate Judiciary Committee. This does not mean, however, that a Senator can dictate an appointment, if the President is determined to prevent it. However, even though the President has the veto power, the nominee must be from a group of candidates acceptable to the Senator.[5]

In the selection of appeals judges, the President and his "men" — the deputy attorney general or the attorney general — can take greater initiative than they can for district judges, because of the multi-state character of the circuits. Justice Department officials to whom the President has delegated much of the initial screening consult friends and colleagues to get suggestions. Nominations must still be cleared with party Senators, and party officials must be consulted when party Senators are lacking, but, in general, the President's men are still very important in appeals court nominations.

Although senatorial domination of judicial selection is a stable and predictable feature of the process, Senators vary widely in the exercise of their prerogatives. Many Senators insist on individual choices even to the point of making demand lists, others will accept nominees if they seem politically and professionally qualified, and still others seem to be uninterested in the power of directing nominations. A few have even suggested alternative methods of judicial selection that would diminish the power of the Senate.

Senators may also vary in their responses to pressures generated at the time of the appointment. The withdrawal of John Morrissey from nomination is an illustration. Because of a pledge President Johnson made to the Kennedys, Senator Edward Kennedy of Massachusetts submitted the name of a family friend and political ally, John Morrissey, for appointment to a district judgeship in Massachusetts. Loud objections were raised by many of the bar associations and mass media when it was revealed that Morrissey obtained his law degree by means of a three-month course in an extension school in Georgia. The objections appeared to be based on the perception of Morrissey as a political crony of the Kennedy family as well as upon the lack of adequate legal qualifications.

Despite the furor of the objections, Morrissey was reported out by the Senate Judiciary Committee and seemed to be in line for ap-

[5] Material on role of the blue slips is taken from the files of the Senate Judiciary Committee.

proval when Senator Kennedy withdrew his name. In this instance, public opinion and the actions of bar associations exercised no direct threat to the approval of the nomination, for it is apparent that Morrissey would have been affirmed if the nomination had not been withdrawn. Public opinion did, however, affect the outcome when Senator Kennedy evidenced concern for his public reputation and political record and decided to rescind the nomination, even after the Senate and President had supported his actions. Other Senators might have been less influenced by the public outcry and persisted in the nomination.[6]

Intervention of Other Actors

In a formal sense, the attorney general has also become a participant in the selection process. He theoretically recommends to the President, in a formal letter, that "John Doe be appointed to the United States District Court for the Western District of Pennsylvania." However, the action of the attorney general is "taken" within the framework of the relevant norms of behavior which operate on the selection process,[7] and rarely does he make independent decisions. Whether or not the attorney general plays more than a formal part in the selection depends partly upon his own interests and partly upon the character of his relationship with the President, for the attorney general is delegated the power to make nominations by the President. At the very least, the attorney general is responsible for a foundation of recommendations and information that varies in importance with the interests and interactions of Senators, state parties, and the President himself. Traditionally, most of the work of processing the nominations has been carried out by the deputy attorney general and his staff, and it is they who are often the visible and formal representatives of the President in the selection process.

Every judicial nomination that clears the initial stages of the selection process is heard by the Senate Judiciary Committee in public hearings. These hearings vary greatly in length, ranging from the perfunctory, ritualistic ceremony of bringing the nominee before the

[6] *The New York Times,* September 28, 1965, p. 6.
[7] Grossman, *Lawyers and Judges,* p. 25.

committee for a few laudatory remarks and supporting testimony, to the kind of searching harassment that lasted for over a year in the nomination of Thurgood Marshall to the court of appeals. As a whole, the hearings do perform an important purpose: they link public opinion to the recruitment process by providing an occasion and an access for the intervention of testimony from the interested public. Witnesses who write to or appear before the committee are a varied lot that includes such persons as lawyer acquaintances, boyhood friends, political opponents of the nominee, judges, Senators other than the sponsoring Senator, civil rights groups, and representatives of state and local bar associations. The committee includes in the record letters and telegrams that have been sent that comment on the nomination. Although there is no proof that such public opinion intervention directly influences approval of an appointment, the hearing does provide access for public opinion to official channels.

The hearings are generally conducted by a subcommittee of three, appointed by the chairman. This subcommittee acts for the committee and issues a recommendation. Ample opportunity is provided for all who express an interest to appear and be heard and occasionally the hearings run to great length.

Legal groups who appear at hearings often express particular interest in the nominee's legal values. Bar groups and lawyers often take interest in such legal traits as the candidate's "judicial temperament," his customary conduct of litigation, and the character of his legal training. Objections were voiced to John Morrissey's improper legal training, as we have seen, and even stronger criticisms were directed by legal groups against the proposed appointment of Irving Ben Cooper to a district judgeship for the Southern District of New York. Judge Cooper (then serving an interim appointment) was nominated by President Kennedy at the suggestion of Representative Emmanuel Celler, who was acting for the Democratic party since both New York Senators were Republicans. The nomination brought vigorous protests from state, city, and national bar associations, and Cooper's poor qualifications were detailed frequently and sometimes at great length, as when the Association of the Bar of the City of New York submitted a thorough brief at the hearing.

Although Cooper's legal training was not disputed, his lack of judicial temperament and his improper conduct of court proceedings were pointed out emphatically. His nomination was also officially opposed by the Committee on the Federal Judiciary of the American Bar Association.[8]

Legal actors sometimes differ, however. An important offset to the legal opposition occurred when Chief Judge Sylvester Ryan, of the court where Ben Cooper was serving an interim appointment, wrote a favorable letter to the committee. In this way the opposition of bar association presidents and of former Attorney General Brownell was countered. The interim appointment of Cooper to the judgeship was an important factor in creating the conditions for support, and, after Judge Ryan's letter commending Cooper's on-the-job record, the committee recommended the nomination and the Senate affirmed without debate.

Both the Cooper and Morrissey cases suggest that although legal groups rarely affect the nomination process directly, they can be important in emphasizing legal values and calling attention to the qualifications of nominees. The Committee on the Federal Judiciary of the American Bar Association has been particularly effective in this regard. Since 1947, the Committee on the Federal Judiciary has customarily ranked all nominees as "exceptionally well qualified," "well qualified," "qualified," or "not qualified," and has sent these rankings to the Senate Judiciary Committee. Although these recommendations have become a regular part of the nomination process, the bar committee does not actually exercise a veto power. In fact, almost 10 per cent of the nominees selected during the Eisenhower and Kennedy administrations were chosen over the objections of the Committee on the Federal Judiciary. The influence of this committee has been, rather, to affect the direction and level of qualifications of candidates for the judiciary. No administration is eager to have many of its appointees labelled as legally unfit, and the Committee on the Federal Judiciary provides a prestigious formal measure of legal qualifications.[9]

---

[8] *Nomination of Irving Ben Cooper,* Hearing before the Committee on the Judiciary, United States Senate, 87th Congress, 2nd Session, March 19–20, 1962.

[9] Grossman, *Lawyers and Judges.*

The members of the sitting judiciary seldom intervene in the selection process by directing attention to legal qualifications of nominees. One major exception was the active part played by Chief Justice Taft during his tenure on the Supreme Court. Taft had unusual prestige and political authority among federal judges because of having been President, because of his active work in the profession of law, and because of his leadership of the Republican party. The chief justice intervened several times in lower court appointments, and he frequently had the ear of the President in his opposition to candidates whom he considered ill-qualified in the law or apt to behave improperly politically, and was thus able to block some nominations. Despite his enormous influence with the administration, Chief Justice Taft was never able to insist on the selection of a candidate he considered especially well qualified. The nomination was thus sometimes given to a candidate who, while acceptable to a Senator, was not his first choice. When Taft's insistence really aroused senatorial ire, however, threats were made that if the Taft policies on appointments were pursued, then the President would not be able to count on the support of a Senator and his party.[10]

There have been rare instances of intervention by lower court judges, as in the case of Judge Ryan, which was discussed above. Another instance occurred in 1952, when Eisenhower nominated Judge Ernest A. Tolin with the approval of the two Republican Senators from California and aroused great controversy in the California Southern District Court. Tolin had received an interim appointment to this district shortly before. Two of his fellow judges from the southern California district opposed his nomination in a letter to the Senate Judiciary Committee, quoting rumors of misconduct and stating that Judge Tolin had neither the reputation nor standing that would qualify him for this position. Despite the divided court, Judge Tolin was affirmed and took his place as a

[10] Walter Murphy, "Chief Justice Taft and the Lower Court Bureaucracy: A Study in Judicial Administration," 24 *Journal of Politics* (1962), pp. 453–476. Also see David J. Danelski, *A Supreme Court Justice is Appointed* (New York: Random House, 1964), and Alpheus T. Mason, *William Howard Taft, Chief Justice* (New York: Simon and Schuster, 1965).

district judge. Given the strained intercourt relationships that must have followed, one can well understand the reluctance of federal judges to intervene in the selection process.[11]

Partisan Backgrounds of Judges

The core process in the selection of the lower federal judiciary strongly suggests the importance of judgeships as components of political party activity in the United States. Table 3 confirms our expectations of the relevance of party in the recruitment of federal judges.

Relevance of Party in Lower Court Appointments, 1884–1962   TABLE 3

President	Percentage of Judicial Appointments from Party of President
Cleveland	100.0 (N = 37)
Harrison	89.7 (N = 29)
McKinley	95.7 (N = 23)
T. Roosevelt	97.2 (N = 72)
Taft	82.2 (N = 35)
Wilson	98.6 (N = 72)
Harding	97.3 (N = 44)
Coolidge	94.1 (N = 68)
Hoover	85.7 (N = 49)
F. Roosevelt	95.9 (N = 194)
Truman	92.8 (N = 125)
Eisenhower	94.8 (N = 174)
Kennedy	92.6 (N = 108)

Source for appointments before Truman: Evan A. Evans, "Political Influence in the Selection of Federal Judges," *Wisconsin Law Review* (1958), pp. 330–351.

All but three of the thirteen Presidents before Johnson have appointed lower federal judiciary from their own party 90 per cent of the time. Two Republican Presidents who fell slightly short of that figure, Taft and Hoover, did so not because of neu-

[11] *Nomination of Ernest A. Tolin,* Hearing before the Committee on the Judiciary, United States Senate, 82nd Congress, 2nd Session, April 17, 1952.

trality, but because there were no Southern Republican candidates for the appointments. During the administration of both, there were few Republican members of the bar in the South and probably fewer still who were sufficiently prominent to merit consideration for judicial appointment.

Party influences are a usual prerequisite for nomination but are complicated by the ambiguities of party ideologies. Although we expect both Democratic and Republican judges to bear their respective imprints of party identification, we would also expect the variation in intra-party values to be reflected in the judiciary. Hence Democratic appointments from the South bring in many conservatives to the lower courts, just as the election of Southern Democratic congressmen brings conservatives to the legislature. As the Congress contains both Democratic-liberal Fulbright and Democratic-conservative Eastland, so have Southern courts had a Democratic-liberal Wright and Democratic-conservative Mize. Party affiliation brings no more ideological uniformity to the courts than it does to the Congress.

Although the senatorial influence in the selection of district judges ranges from an absolute veto at the minimum to an absolute choice at the maximum, the range of choice is more circumscribed in the selection of appeals judges. The multi-state constituencies of the appellate courts decisively weaken the power of senatorial courtesy, because no one Senator or pair of Senators can claim an exclusive interest in the appointments. Although the judges are informally apportioned out among the states in the circuit, Senators must wait their turn in making their views significant until there is an appointment that is understood to go to their particular state. The President and his advisors decide on both the order of allocation of judges to particular states and the specific pattern of allocation among the states of the circuit. Senators have some say about apointments, but it is clear that the balance of power is in the hands of the presidential party.

The appointment of former Governor J. P. Coleman of Mississippi to a post on the Fifth Circuit is, however, an indication of residual power of Senators over court of appeals appointments. The vacancy occurred as a result of the death of Judge Ben Cameron, a long-time conservative on civil rights. Since Cameron was from Mississippi and since the other five Southern states already had judges on the court, it was assumed that the nominee would be a Mississippian. This assumption was greatly strengthened by the fact that the chairman of the Senate Judiciary Committee, Senator Eastland, was from Mississippi. Coleman was the choice of the Mississippi Senators, and his nomination was affirmed despite his unfavorable civil rights record and over the protests of civil rights groups.

The Coleman appointment exemplifies an accurate prediction of how appointees will behave on the bench. As governor of Mississippi, Coleman had led that state in its opposition to civil rights, but in the context of Mississippi politics he was known as a moderate. Civil rights groups opposed his nomination because of his largely successful fight against the extension of civil rights, but many people viewed him as more desirable than most of his state colleagues because of his moderation. His selection illustrates a presidential dilemma, for, despite his anti-civil rights record, Coleman was the only "moderate" of any stature who was acceptable to the Senators from the state.

In an *en banc* decision handed down shortly after his appointment, Coleman confirmed the accuracy of the opposition's fears by joining the conservative faction on the Fifth Circuit to vote against the civil rights position in a crucial case involving the systematic desegregation of schools in the South.[12] Thus, the civil rights groups who viewed his appointment with dismay were correct in predicting that he would vote with the anti-civil rights bloc on the court.

The Importance of Localism

Considered alone, the general selection process shown in Table 1 admits a large and varied population of candidates to nomination for the lower court judiciary. Closer inspection of the selection process, however, indicates that only a relatively small group of persons are ever "considered" as possible nominees, and that a large number of persons are somehow ruled out of consideration. Our models of

[12] *Caddo Parish School Board v. United States,* March 29, 1967.

judicial selection suggest that a kind of screening process eliminates candidates with clearly unsuitable traits and admits those with desirable characteristics. We have examined the impact of partisan screening and now turn to an examination of the influence of localism upon the recruitment process.

A persistent factor in the molding of lower court organization has been the preservation of state and regional boundaries. The feeling that the judiciary should reflect the local features of the federal system has often been expressed by state officials most explicitly. Mississippi congressman John Sharp Williams declared that he was "frankly opposed to a perambulatory judiciary, to carpetbagging Nebraska with a Louisianian, certainly to carpetbagging Mississippi or Louisiana with somebody north of Mason and Dixon's line." [13]

The probability of local influence is built into the selection system through the operation of senatorial patronage. In addition, selection officials may well respond to important values in the political culture by emphasizing the value of local experience and background in the choice of judges to represent particular constituencies. For example, nearly all congressmen "come from" the district they represent in the sense that their past experiences have identified them with the district from which they are elected. Although recruitment for the judiciary is different than that for Congress, the traditions and the structure of the federal courts suggest a similar concern for localism in recruitment.

Although we cannot assume that local origins necessarily bring local values and behaviors to those recruited, we do know that there is a popular assumption that the relationship exists and that this belief influences recruitment patterns. Moreover, differences in the experiences and social backgrounds of officials can be useful in assessing differences in behavior.

The data in Table 4 offer clues about the geographical origins of district judges. Quite likely the figure of 57.7 per cent underestimates the proportion of judges who "come from" the district of their court appointment, since many doubtless moved into the district during childhood or in later life. Nevertheless, the figures

---

[13] Quoted in Felix Frankfurter and James M. Landis, *The Business of the Supreme Court* (New York: Macmillan, 1927), p. 239.

are a crude estimate of the importance of localism as a factor in the selection of district judges and show that more than half the district judges are identified with the district court they serve.

Localism in the Backgrounds
of District Judges, 1963   TABLE 4

Background of Judge	Percentage
Born in district of court	57.7 (N = 234)
Born in state of court	66.6 (N = 234)
Educated at law school in	
same state as court	60.5 (N = 228)

N(numbers) vary because of differences in availability of data. Data derived from *Who's Who, Directory of Judges,* and files of Senate Judiciary Committee.

In a similar way, appeals judges are often identified with the regional geographical and educational facilities in the circuits. The information in Table 5 indicates that the regions contained within the circuits are effective limitations upon some of the background features of the judges who are recruited for the appeals courts. The regional limitations do not suggest the same local limitations that district court selection does, but they do show that sectional limitations are important. For judicial constituencies, data of this sort is less significant than it would be for legislative districts, which are usually smaller and thus more specialized and numerous within the states. In some instances, judicial districts are coterminous with state boundaries, while this occurs seldom with congressional dis-

Regionalism in the Backgrounds
of Appeals Judges, 1963   TABLE 5

Background of Judge	Percentage
Born in state of circuit	77.1 (N = 73)
Educated at law school in	
same state of the circuit	86.4 (N = 72)

Data derived from the same sources as data in Table 4.

tricts. In no case is a state divided into more than four judicial districts, whereas legislative districts are sometimes ten times more numerous in populous states.

There are several reasons why recruitment of judges from the vicinity of the constituency may be of political significance. Since both district and appeals judges frequently receive legal training in the state or circuit they serve, the significance of legal education is important. If a federal judge is trained at a state university, he is exposed to and may assimilate state and sectional political viewpoints, especially since state law schools are training grounds for local political elites. Attendance at a private university in the vicinity can still provide contact with local values, but may also provide a more cosmopolitan student body and an environment that is more distant from the state political system than the state university law school. Other than education, different local environments provide different reactions to policy issues, such as civil rights or labor relations. Indeed, throughout the history of the lower court judiciary there is evidence that various persons involved in judicial organization and selection have perceived that local, state, or regional factors make a difference and have behaved accordingly. Finally, we know that in other political institutions such as the legislature, local, state, and regional features mold political behavior and lead to variations in decision making.

Legal Training and Experiences

The federal judiciary, in addition to its political relationships, has explicit linkage to the legal culture. Although a large number of legislators have been lawyers, and although traditional legal forms are used in the conduct of legislative business, legalistic influences pervade the judiciary in much more profound fashion both in the cognitive and the evaluative aspects of institutional behavior. Legal groups can be expected to try to influence the selection process of the judiciary, even though politicians dominate regular recruitment procedures.

Legal groups try to exert control by insisting on legal training, because of the implicit assumption that legal training will bring some grasp of legal values. The growing professionalization of law and the greater emphasis on formal training have not only made more legal education possible, but have also contributed to the expectation that legal actors should possess formal legal training. The extent of this training in the federal judiciary has developed in the district courts as shown in Table 6. As recently as 1930 about half of all judges did not have law degrees, but within one generation, the number of federal judiciary selected without formal legal training has grown smaller and doubtless will largely disappear in the appointment of future judges.

Percentage of District Judges
Without Law Degrees   TABLE 6

Sitting in 1930	46.2
Sitting in 1962	8.9
Selected since 1945	5.6

We are indebted to Joel Grossman for allowing us access to his data here and elsewhere.

No development reflects the emphasis on legal education as pointedly as does the inclusion of the American Bar Association Committee on the Federal Judiciary in the selection process. The rating system applied to every nominee has doubtless increased public awareness of legal qualifications and directed attention to variations in legal education, even though the ratings are apparently based on a number of characteristics other than quality of legal training. As a matter of fact, the American Bar Association committee has never announced explicitly what it considers the qualifications of a good judge. Since there are many roles and occupations in the legal profession, the committee would probably have difficulty reaching a criterion acceptable to all. Only regarding candidates educated in obviously marginal law facilities such as correspondence or "quickie," "degree-mill" type schools has the committee made its position clear, as in the Morrissey case.[14] We have noted that Morrissey's

[14] Grossman, *Lawyers and Judges,* p. 201.

judicial experience as municipal court judge did not seem to compensate in the minds of his legal opponents for the absence of a *bona fide* law degree.

Legal experience is, however, valued as a quality that should be present in a good judge — at least, this seems to be so in the legal literature, especially in the pages of the *Journal of the American Judicature Society*. "Judicial experience" includes a variety of legal experiences. Adjudication experience in lower federal courts or in state courts is most frequently cited as a desirable qualification for appeals courts; adjudication in state and local courts is similarly cited for district courts. Non-judicial legal experience includes being counsel for government agencies, district attorney, trial lawyer, and law teacher, although the latter is not usually regarded as a practical kind of legal experience. There is considerable ambiguity about which experiences are best or most proper for qualification. Since the American Bar Association has never explicitly stated its preferred experiences, its liaison activities with the attorney general are based upon deliberately unstated norms for the nomination of candidates. Legislation has been introduced in Congress requiring five to ten years prior judicial experience on the part of Supreme Court appointees, but none has been enacted, and no accepted standard has emerged for judicial qualification.

Table 7 shows the percentage of lower court judges with previous judicial experience. About one out of three judges in the district courts, slightly more in the appeals courts, and slightly fewer in the district courts possesses previous judicial experience. Despite the increased intervention of legal groups in the selection process, the frequency of judicial experience for nominees has not increased significantly over the past two decades. Since the appointment of

Percentage of Judges Having Previous Judicial Experience   TABLE 7

District judges	31.0
Appeals judges	38.7

Data derived from same sources as data in Table 4.

persons with previous judicial experience is a kind of in-service promotion there are other reasons why we might expect it to occur more frequently than it actually does. In adjudication the judge is visible to legal and political groups, and his skills and performance record can be easily discovered. His actual judicial qualifications are thus easily available for consideration. To the extent that judicial skills are recognizable and can be communicated, there should be, it would seem, a larger amount of intra-judicial promotion.

Examination of past judicial records can yield, among other things, insight into such qualities as "judicial temperament" and the ability to handle technical problems and complicated litigation. But although there is some agreement on who the great judges are, lower court judicial performance cannot be easily and reliably evaluated. The published hearings of the Senate Judiciary Committee reveal few instances in which judicial performances have been evaluated in the consideration of nominations. In the case of Judge Irving Ben Cooper, discussed above, bar groups and individuals did go to considerable trouble to prove that Cooper had behaved improperly as a judge. The Association of the Bar of the City of New York, in order to demonstrate the absence of judicial temperament, listed such characteristics as "sudden almost uncontrollable fits of temper and emotional outbursts; harassment of lawyers . . . false pride resulting in prejudice to the due administration of justice." [15] Judge Ryan's contradictory testimony and Cooper's eventual confirmation, however, indicate how difficult it is to assess judicial performance when there are few agreed upon standards.

The selection of appeals judges is an excellent test of the prevelance of internal judicial promotion. It is possible that state and local judges may not be visible in their on-the-bench performances, but federal district judges gain more attention. District judges write opinions in cases, some of which are appealed to the Supreme Court; they often hear cases that gain public attention; and the litigation in their courts often involves political officials. Reflecting their judicial behaviors, district judges frequently become judicial personalities in their own right. About

[15] *Nomination of Irving Ben Cooper,* p. 370.

two-fifths of the appeals judges sitting in 1963 had been lower court judges before their appointments, and 91.0 per cent of this number had been federal district judges. That is to say, about one-third of appeals courts appointments are made from the district courts. Thus, while inter-court promotion is more frequent in the appeals courts than in other federal courts, it is by no means an efficient means of recognizing and rewarding judicial behaviors in the districts. The rather modest amount of in-service promotion, from district to appeals court, is possible, indeed, only because of the increased influence of the President in the selection process and the decreased impact of senatorial courtesy.

All but 1.5 per cent of district judges had practiced law and had spent time in private practice ranging up to forty years and averaging fifteen years. At the time of their appointment, almost half the district judges (48.7 per cent), but only 21.0 per cent of the appeals judges, were practicing law as their main occupation. Table 8 shows the legal experience gained in other judicial offices besides judgeships — including district attorney, assistant district attorney, special government counsel, clerk of court, and city, county, or state attorney.

Percentage Who Have Held
Other Judicial Office   TABLE 8

	Federal Offices	State Offices
District judges	21.8	41.2
Appeals judges	46.4	25.2

Data derived from same sources as data in Table 4.

Clearly, a significant proportion of the judiciary have held legal office under either the state or national governments. It can be argued that such experiences are superior to private practice as preparation for the role of federal judge. Besides providing practical experience, legal service in government provides exposure to many political issues. The experiences gained are thus more frequently relevant to the major issues and conflicts of law that the judicial appointee will encounter on the bench. Some such point of view is doubtless behind the tendencies of the President to choose nominees with federal experience and of Senators to choose nominees with state experience. If we combine all the varieties of judicial experience, about three-fourths of the federal judges have had judicial experience, either on the bench or as a government representative in the courtroom.

There is evidence that the process of selection may be gradually undergoing modification. Because of the institutionalized role of the American Bar Association in the selection process, more attention has been given in recent nominations to professional legal traits. In consequence, the attorney general's evaluation of nominations has taken on added significance, and the role of the Senators in the selection process has become less absolute than before. One survey of forty Senators indicated that 55 per cent of them thought it a good idea to consult with the Department of Justice and the American Bar Association committee before publicly announcing their choice for nomination, and 18 per cent favored the idea that Senators should submit a list of names to the Department of Justice rather than a single name.[16] Considered against the traditional importance of senatorial courtesy in partisan politics, these replies represent a sharp break with traditional attitudes.

Judicial selection remains perhaps the chief battleground of the legal and democratic cultures. Although the federal judiciary has escaped the effects of popular election and Jacksonian direct democracy which swept through the state judiciary, it nevertheless contains important elements of the democratic culture: judicial recruitment reflects and helps institutionalize partisan changes; it serves the needs and demands of a diverse federal system; it links the Senate to local party structures; and it helps soften the impact of the extension of national power to the states. These political functions, often expressed and practiced in common democratic fashion, have outraged the legalistic sensibilities of some important legal actors. One commented acidly that "inferior judgeships are

---

[16] Grossman, *Lawyers and Judges,* p. 132.

treated as party pie . . . and worse is the fact that these judgeships have come to be regarded as jobs to be handed out at the behest of local party chiefs." And Dean Wigmore declared flatly, "The time has come to abolish . . . these unconstitutional practices. The Constitution never meant that the Senators should nominate." [17]

The impact of the legal culture upon judicial selection will probably continue to be indirect and advisory rather than directly influential, despite the continuing recommendations of legalists to the contrary. The recruitment of federal judges is too important to the values of the democratic culture to be abandoned to nonpolitical participants.

[17] Quoted in Harris, *Advice and Consent of the Senate,* p. 315.

DECISION MAKING
IN THE DISTRICT COURTS

As the first and only courts that most litigants in the federal system see, the district courts occupy a fundamental position in the federal judiciary. These courts not only receive the great mass of federal cases, but they also settle in final form the great majority of cases decided in the federal courts. This latter point may be illustrated by reference to the year 1960 in which 93.8 per cent of all cases filed in the federal courts were settled in final form at the district level. But important as district courts are in settling cases, they also handle quite a few cases that are later appealed. A large part of the Supreme Court's work and most of the litigation of the appeals courts are cases that have initially been decided by district courts. Because of this, district court cases constitute the decisional building blocks on which much of the work of the appellate courts depend. From several points of view, therefore, the judicial behavior in the

CHAPTER FIVE

district courts and the character of decision making there, is of great importance in determining the politics of the federal judiciary.

In this chapter, we examine several important phases of district court decision making. These include access to the courts, the screening of claims, the consideration of demands, and judicial behavior. Besides describing patterns of decision making we also consider how decisions are shaped by influences from the legal and democratic subcultures. In every aspect of district court politics the imprints of legal and popular pressures are visible.

Access to the Courts

The decision making potential of the district courts depends initially upon the access by which interests gain entrance into the courts.

Although such factors as motivations and means are also important in determining who gets into the courts, entrance depends to a large extent upon fulfillment of jurisdictional requirements that specify who may make demands upon the courts and under what conditions. Because jurisdiction is defined by the Constitution and acts of Congress, both democratic and legalistic pressures have influenced its contents. It is implemented and applied to specific cases, however, by district judges, acting within formal legal procedures. Although these formal procedures facilitate requests for access by standardizing the procedure, they also make access more impersonal and routine than in some other governmental agencies that establish access through more informal and personalized interactions between decision maker and claimant.

One should not conclude, however, that the formal, legalistic aspects of jurisdiction make access more difficult. On the contrary, the large number of cases filed in the district courts indicates that interests have little difficulty in submitting claims to these courts. In 1960, for example, there were 87,421 cases [1] filed in the district courts, and there was a backlog of 71,523 cases pending from previous filings. Quite clearly, district courts, in common with other political institutions, are responding to the increasing demands of modern society. Indeed, since 1948 the number of claims filed has increased at an annual rate of about 4 per cent.

Although there are several special courts in the judicial system that initially hear cases, the district courts are courts of first instance for most federal litigation. The scope of their involvement in the settlement of disputes is indicated by the breadth of their jurisdiction. Admission to the district courts is gained by interests who bring claims under one of the following categories of jurisdiction: [2]

[1] These and all subsequent data on district court activities, unless otherwise noted, are taken from: *Annual Report of the Director of the Administrative Office of the United States Courts, 1960* (Washington: United States Government Printing Office, 1961). The year 1960 was chosen for the analysis of district court activities because of the more complete statistical data available for that year.

[2] Charles Alan Wright, *Federal Courts* (St. Paul: West Publishing Co., 1963), pp. 64–104. Another standard reference work for the federal courts is Henry M. Hart, Jr., and Herbert Wechsler, *The Federal Courts and the Federal System* (Brooklyn: The Foundation Press, Inc., 1953).

(1) Claims involving bankruptcy, patent, or copyright laws of the United States.

(2) Conflicts arising under the United States Constitution, a law or treaty of the United States, or conflicts involving such a law in a substantial way.

(3) Claims in which the contending parties to the case have diversity of citizenship, that is, are citizens of different states.

(4) Cases arising under diversity of citizenship or under a federal question, and where there is a financial amount involved, with the amount in controversy in excess of $10,000.

While the above categories restrict the issues that may be brought to the courts, they also establish the potential the judiciary has for intervention in American politics. One of the important features of district court jurisdiction is that it opens the way for consideration of national political questions by federal institutions located within the states. A further significance is that problems of national policy can be resolved within the local environments in which they are generated. As a result the courts deal with such diverse subjects as anti-trust regulation, transportation of stolen cars, social security, and labor disputes, within state confines. The courts themselves are a rich source for future cases by their interpretation of the Constitution as illustrated by the numerous school desegregation disputes which arose under the Fourteenth Amendment and the flood of appeals for habeas corpus writs from state and federal prisoners invoking the Fifth and Fourteenth Amendments. The courts continue to be the mainspring of such litigation because both school desegregation and prisoner habeas corpus cases were the direct result of policies enunciated by them.

Another consequence of district court jurisdiction is that it extends the power of the courts into what are essentially local issues through the "diversity of citizenship" and "federal question" types of cases. Any claimants who can arrange diversity of citizenship or can cast their claims in the guise of a "federal question" are able to command the jurisdiction of the district courts.

Still another outcome of district court jurisdiction is the assumption of some aspects of general jurisdiction. While the district courts are not formally courts of general jurisdiction, their wide-ranging activities under diversity of citizenship and federal question clauses enables them to perform some of these courts' functional equivalents. These confer a wide-ranging jurisdiction upon the district courts by extending their activities deeply into state and local politics, and by including cases that have little linkage with national issues. The diversity cases make possible general access to the federal courts because they admit matters that satisfy geographical and financial requirements without any further restriction on subject matter or the character of the litigants. In the diversity cases the courts handle no distinctive group of legal issues but deal concurrently with matters handled by state courts. These cases can include such issues as automobile accident liability, breaches of contract, damage suits against airlines, insurance disputes, and many others that have no specific origins in the Constitution, laws, or treaties of the United States.[3] In a similar manner federal question cases may deal with local issues pursued by community litigants who gain access to the federal courts by raising a federal question — often on a subsidiary issue — which may concern a constitutional issue or a provision of a federal law.

Both diversity and federal question aspects of federal court jurisdiction result in an ambiguous access to the courts that has the effect of injecting an element of choice in litigants' presentation of their claims. That is, the same case may be eligible for entrance into either state or federal courts, depending on how litigants perceive and present the case. It is clear that considerable manipulation takes place in meeting the requirements for diversity of citizenship, for the size of the financial stake, and for defining the existence of a federal question. For example, in a breach of contract suit involving persons from different states, the claimant can remain in state court by keeping the claim below $10,000. The choice of courts may be important because certain kinds of litigation, such as civil rights cases, have a reputation for being heard more favorably in the federal courts and others, such as suits against insurance companies, are said to receive more favorable treatment by state judges and juries.

[3] Wright, *Federal Courts,* pp. 64–72.

Initial Screening of Demands

Because the judiciary must admit all claimants who satisfy jurisdictional requirements and meet relatively simple legal procedures,
the district courts are presented with a great mass of case filings for
their consideration each year. The scope of the problem may be
illustrated by 1960 when the cases filed averaged 386.8 cases per
district judge. In an institution in which decision making on a
single issue often consumes several weeks, for example in income
tax and anti-trust cases, a load of this magnitude apparently presents
serious problems. But the effects of these numerous demands are not
as serious as they seem, for the courts have evolved processes to
handle the large number of claims made upon them. A critical
factor in judicial decision making is the control courts exercise over
the flow of decisions. Although the popular picture is that claims
made in the courts are settled by full trial, the actuality is that
procedures have been developed by courts to dispose of most of the
claims without resorting to full hearing. These legal procedures constitute a preliminary screening process by which the judiciary is able
to dispose of most cases with less time and energy than would be
required in a full trial. Decisions made in these screening procedures
as to which issues and litigants merit more extensive consideration
often embody important policy values by the court. A breakdown
of these preliminary methods of screening is revealed in Table 1.

More than half the cases were settled with no active participation
by the court. They were withdrawn, abandoned, or settled by private
agreement of the litigating parties. A small group, amounting to
4.1 per cent, was taken out of court after being transferred to other
courts or agencies, consolidated with existing litigation, or settled
routinely through remand processes from higher courts. Almost
one-third (29.4 per cent) involved activity of the district judge but
were settled by processes other than conventional decision making.
Only 10.3 per cent required a trial for settlement, and not all of
these required a full trial.

When motions are made by contesting parties to dismiss the case
or to render a directed verdict, the judge is involved in the decision

Methods of Case Disposition in
the District Courts, 1960   TABLE 1

Disposition	Percentage of All Cases
By consent with no motion made and no pretrial	56.2
After pre-trial or motion made	18.0
By court on contested motion before trial	11.4
Trial or after trial began	10.3
Other dispositions such as transfers, remands, or consolidations	4.1
	100.0

Source: See footnote 1.

but without the substance of an accompanying trial. Decisions on motions doubtless involve discretionary behavior on the part of the judge and may involve issues of great impact, but such decisions are not individually recorded. Such reports are consequently not durable records of judicial behavior. Moreover, these dispositions require less time on the part of the judge and allow him to dispose of a greater load of litigation.

Pre-trial dispositions of litigation have become an especially important form of decision making in the district court, supplementing in many important respects the traditional ways of deciding cases. In 1960 over 15,000 pre-trial conferences were held, and in 6,126 of these decisions were made that settled the cases.

Specifically authorized by the Code of Civil Procedure, pre-trial conferences differ substantially from the usual trial methods. In general, the procedure involves consultation with lawyers in the judge's chambers and an attempt through informal discussions to reach a specific decision in the case; in some instances, the objective is to agree on evidence and major legal points, thus simplifying and shortening the trial. Though many judges use the pre-trial conference simply as a means of preparation for the trial, others use it as an explicit form of decision making. The use of pre-trial proceedings is entirely discretionary with individual judges, and there is wide variation among the district courts in both the frequency and the character of its usage. For example, a survey of use of pre-trial procedures in the western district of Pennsylvania indicates that judges differed in the amount of pre-trial processes used, in the character of cases selected for pre-trial, and in the importance pre-trials received as a method of disposition.[4] In this survey, Judge Miller entered a pre-trial order in all cases and held them sometimes in open court and sometimes in chambers, whereas Judge Sorg used them only in negligence jury cases and in anti-trust cases where no jury was involved.

The informal nature of the proceedings gives, moreover, ample scope for the expression of different decision making orientations. In addition, the district judge is afforded the opportunity of making a final decision and, because the decision is not formally noted and the proceeding not recorded in the usual way, to take the decision out of the appellate process and end matters. An outstanding example of this usage may be observed in the activities of Judge Skelly Wright of the Eastern District of Louisiana, who used the pre-trial conference as a channel for his own variety of "judicial activism."[5]

So important have been the conferences in settling disputes and screening cases that the Judicial Conference has considered the creation of special pre-trial examiners who would assist the district judge in his work. In the meantime, the Judicial Conference encourages the use of pre-trial conferences by holding special seminars on their administration and by giving them a great deal of attention in other ways. Their usage is one of the means by which district judges clear their dockets and conserve their time and energies for other policy work.

By the use of pre-trial conferences and other methods the district courts manage to screen out the great majority of litigation filed before it actually reaches trial. Figures on court congestion that deal simply with cases filed or cases pending are thus unrealistic esti-

[4] Fannie J. Klein, *Survey of the U.S. District Court Western District of Pennsylvania* (Washington: Administrative Office of the United States Courts, February, 1960), pp. 25–29.

[5] Herbert Jacob, *Justice in America* (Boston: Little, Brown, 1965), p. 84.

mates. Most cases are terminated with little judicial activity and many of the remainder concluded without a full trial.

Although the enormous number of cases filed would suggest that the district judiciary is immobilized, our analysis indicates that the judges manage to dispose of the great majority of cases short of trial and are able to concentrate on a relatively few cases. Because of this a reasonable hypothesis is that controversial and possibly important cases probably receive about as much attention in the district judiciary as do important policies in other political institutions.

Full Consideration of Demands

Decision making in the district courts by full trials takes two forms, trial by jury and trial by judge. The two methods of trial represent quite different kinds of decision making for they involve contrasting elements of the legal and democratic subcultures, cast the district judge in dissimilar roles, and embody quite different varieties of decisional behavior. Although both are frequently used in the district courts, they have different effects on the politics of the lower courts.

In 1960, out of 9,998 cases that were tried in the district courts, 55.4 per cent were heard by juries (71.3 per cent of all criminal cases and 47.1 per cent of all civil cases). Right to trial by jury is guaranteed by the Constitution's Seventh Amendment in "suits at common law where the value in controversy shall exceed twenty dollars" and by provisions in certain federal statutes. If the case satisfies jurisdictional requirements, a jury trial may be obtained on demand of one litigant and if the claim is "legal" rather than "equitable," that is, if it concerns such common actions as tort claims or breach of contract. If jury trial is waived or if the case involves an "equitable" action such as an injunction or writ of specific performance, the case is heard by the district judge or, in a few instances, by a three-judge court.[6]

The frequency of jury trials is a measure of the strength of democratic values in district court decision making. In jury trials

[6] Wright, *Federal Courts,* pp. 350–356.

cases are decided by a group of decision makers drawn directly from the district locality and with no specified expertness or experience in the law. Although district judges often have community attachments, we would expect district juries to have even stronger and more direct links with local public opinion and interests. Litigants, by controlling the way by which a case comes to court and by requesting or waiving the right to a jury trial, are frequently able to choose between judge and jury. Because of their closer links to the democratic subculture, juries are popularly thought to be more favorable to certain values than judges and the choice of decision maker sometimes becomes an important issue in the district courts. For instance labor groups have thought district judges to be unsympathetic to the cause of labor, and the usual preference of injured parties for juries in suits involving workmen's compensation, insurance claims, and consumers' rights is well known.

An example of such preference occurs in civil rights cases in the South. Although in the Deep South it may make little immediate difference whether a segregation-minded district judge or jury hears the case, civil rights advocates would generally rather have their case decided by the local federal judge. Their suspicions have been borne out by the recent instances in which Southern juries have refused to convict defendants in civil rights criminal cases; district judges would doubtless have decided upon conviction more frequently. However, it is erroneous to suppose that federal judges and juries act separately, for, in certain phases of jury trials, judge and jury interact. Some critics have charged that federal judges, through their control over the selection and administration of juries in their courts, make certain that it is impossible to get a fair trial in certain areas of the Deep South. On the other hand, Judge Frank Johnson of the middle district court of Alabama has shown that a determined judge can lead Southern juries into convictions in these kinds of cases.[7]

The decisional values of juries are particularly important because jury decisions are not as open to appeal as are judge-made decisions. Issues of fact decided by juries are not appealable and the jury's decision can be appealed only if the judge handles a jury trial in

[7] *Time*, May 12, 1967, pp. 72–78.

such a way as to create a point of law. Although quite a few jury trials are appealed on the issue of the presiding judge's conduct, usually the judge's handling of the case creates no legal or constitutional issues and the jury decision prevails without review. Jury trials have the effect, therefore, of maximizing democratic values in the districts and of minimizing modification of local values by appellate review.

Despite the importance attached to jury trials, nearly half of all cases tried in the district courts are heard by the district judge acting alone. Collectively, district judges in 1960 presided over 5,538 jury trials (an average of 24.5 per judge) and decided 4,461 cases (an average of 19.5 per judge). It is the twenty or so cases that the judge decides that are his most conspicuous contribution to the district court. These decisions are usually published,[8] become part of the body of federal law, and establish the public image of the judge, and, to a large extent, of the district courts.

Judge-made decisions in the districts, although they often reflect local orientations, provide more extensive linkages with the legal subculture than do jury trials. As a member of legal groups such as a bar association and the judicial council, the district judge is associated with legal interests that are concerned with the district courts. Unlike the deliberations of the jury, his decisions are couched in the language and structured in the rationale learned in his legal training. Moreover, all the district judges' decisions are appealable to regional appellate courts and, potentially, to the Supreme Court.

[8] Rules 52 and 58 of the Federal Rules of Civil Procedure state that in all nonjury cases the court shall "state separately its conclusions of law" and that every judgment "shall be set forth on a separate document." These provisions call for publication of all nonjury decisions in the district courts, and it would seem that the normal procedure is for publication of district court decisions. Certainly, all cases that are potentially appealable call for writing and publication in order to be available for the appellate process. One authority has suggested, however, in a careful discussion of the problem, that not all district cases may be published. The decentralized and localized character of district court organization and administration contribute some support for such a hypothesis. See Kenneth M. Dolbeare, "The Federal District Courts and Urban Public Policy: An Exploratory Study (1960–67)," in Joel Grossman and Joseph Tanenhaus, eds., *Frontiers of Judicial Research* (New York: John Wiley and Sons, 1969), pp. 377–378.

Through appellate review, judges' decisional values are thus subject to the inspection and modification of other judicial officials.

Although most opinions are written by individual judges, in a small number of instances a three-judge court is convened to decide cases in the district judiciary. Instituted by statute in 1910, the practice of convening three-judge district courts was originally intended to mitigate the power of federal courts in challenging state laws. Congress believed that a three-judge court, composed of one circuit judge and two district judges, would provoke less public resentment in staying the enforcement of state statutes. The original act has been amended to include injunctions against acts of Congress claimed to be unconstitutional. A further provision is that three-judge cases bypass the appeals courts and convey a right for appeal directly to the Supreme Court.[9]

Three-judge courts are not identified with a particular locality because the composition of the panel mixes district and appellate judges from different constituencies. It is clear that this kind of court is not as closely linked to the localistic elements of the democratic subculture as are many district courts.

Staff Participation in Decisions

The district judge carries on his work in relative isolation within the district. Almost two-thirds of the districts have one or two judges, and about one-third have only one judge. Even in multiple judge districts, the judges are sometimes split up by assignment to hold court in separate divisions. Though often without judicial companionship, each district judge has substantial assistance from nonjudicial personnel.

The staff attached to each court is the means by which district judges deal with major work loads and manage the judicial process efficiently. The various stages of the judicial process are implemented by such officials as the United States commissioner, who holds preliminary hearings, a clerical staff that handles research and processing, bailiffs who manage bail problems, and special staffs which render *ad hoc* assistance.

[9] Wright, *Federal Courts*, pp. 161–167.

The work of staff members seldom conflicts with the values of the district judge; more often it reflects and extends them. Not only does the judge influence staff work by his presence in the court, but his power of personnel selection gives him indirect control.

Although normally the activities of such court personnel as the United States commissioners and bailiffs are not publicized, doubtless these officials respond to important social and political features of their environment. On occasion, the prominence of one of the cases in which such officials are involved will focus attention upon the political character of their actions. Such an occasion occurred in 1964 in the court for the southern district of Mississippi in a nationally publicized case involving the murder of civil right workers.[10] At a hearing before United States Commissioner Esther Carter, an FBI agent testified that he had a signed confession implicating a group of local persons, including community law enforcement officials. Commissioner Carter ruled, however, that the confession was inadmissible as evidence and dismissed the charges.

Commissioner Carter had been appointed to her post in 1961 by District Judge Sidney Mize, an inveterate opponent of Negro civil rights, whose decisions usually went against such rights. Before that, Carter had been a deputy clerk of court in the same court and, in addition, was a long-time member of the community where the civil rights murders occurred. During the hearing Commissioner Carter, who was not a lawyer, was given legal advice by Judge Mize's law clerk. Her action in dismissing the case was widely criticized on the grounds that it violated accepted standards in not bringing charges against individuals against whom law enforcement officials had evidence. Technically, however, the action, illegal and unwise as it may have been, was within the discretion of her office.

A Sample of District Decisions

For our exploration of decision making in the district courts we went directly to the cases and drew a sample of them for analysis. Our sample included all civil liberties and labor cases from the 33

[10] *The New York Times,* December 11, 1964, pp. 1, 34.

district courts of the Third, Fifth, and Eighth Circuits decided during the years 1956 to 1961. These cases were selected because they involved policy questions of an unusually important, sensitive, and interesting nature. We chose the district courts of the Third, Fifth, and Eighth Circuits because they constituted a wide geographic distribution. The Fifth contains courts of the Deep South, the Third a combination of Middle Atlantic and New England industrial states, and the Eighth a combination of Middle Western states and Arkansas.

The character of judicial institutions thus represented is varied, including contrasting social and economic characteristics which are captured within the district boundaries. The range of districts that we have included varies from the southern Mississippi district, with practically no urban and industrial development and a high Negro population, to the western district of Pennsylvania, which is highly urbanized and industrialized and has an average Negro population. In partisan characteristics, the districts range from the Democratic area of western Pennsylvania to the traditionally Republican area of Nebraska, and from the conservative districts of Mississippi to the competitive, partisan districts of New Jersey. The number and location of cases in our sample is shown in Table 2.

The District as a Decision Making Variable

The constituencies of district court activity are clearly not simply passive containers of judicial activity. They constitute the environment within which decisions take place, and they mold, as we have shown, both the character of the judges that are selected and the nature of district court institutions.

The lack of centralization and coordination in the districts ensures that the individuality of the separate districts is maintained. Each district is a separate, largely self-contained political unit with little administrative relation to the other districts and little direction and coordination from above. For example, before lawyers may practice before a district court, they must qualify to practice before that particular court. Judge Gordon West of Louisiana, angry critic of many civil rights policies, refused to allow United

Number and Location of Cases in Sample   TABLE 2

| District Cases | Number of Cases | | |
from	Labor	Civil Liberties	Total
Third Circuit	288	163	451
Fifth Circuit	127	130	257
Eighth Circuit	64	68	132
All	479	361	840

States Attorney General Robert Kennedy to participate in civil rights suits in his court until he qualified to practice in the Baton Rouge division court. On such a routine matter as reporting of cases, the district courts report judicial statistics mainly according to their own criteria and conform to few central standards. Thus, within the limits of the district system, each court determines its own style and character of litigation. There is no problem of field and central office relationships as is found in administrative organizations, for there is no central agency and no administrative official responsible for directing and integrating the work of the district courts. The Administrative Office of the Courts is limited largely to the collection of statistics, and the Judicial Conference, as we have said before, has failed to assume supervisory functions over the court system.

Among the districts that we have included for analysis, the amount of litigation is unequal both in terms of total cases handled and in the character of litigation. The reasons for varying amounts of litigation are complicated, but certain major relationships that influence the variation are evident. Two general factors frequently cited as stimulating litigation are population and the degree of urbanism. To these two factors we have added the number of judges, as a rough measure of size of judicial facility, and have investigated their impact upon the amount of litigation in both labor and civil liberties cases. The results are shown in Table 3.

Both total population and urban population are related to the amount of litigation in the districts by moderately large correlations, although neither factor accounts for much more than about half the variation. Undoubtedly, the number of judges overlaps with

*Correlation of Certain District Features
              with Amount of Litigation*   TABLE 3

| District Feature | All Cases Filed | Types of Cases | |
		Labor	Civil Liberties
Total population	.77	.60	.67
Population in cities			
over 50,000	.84	.68	.64
Number of judges	.76	.81	.80

Source: Data here and in subsequent tables from sample survey of cases and from United States census. Correlations are Pearsonian product moment.

the factors of both urbanism and population, but there is a slight suggestion that size of judicial facility is related to amount of litigation. It is obvious that some variables other than the ones investigated help determine the amount of litigation in the districts.

Inspection of litigation in certain districts in Table 4 illustrates the relationships described in Table 3 and emphasizes the differences even in districts of the same region.

In the same region there are sharp contrasts in decision making activity among district courts because litigation is sparse in some courts, such as that of southern Mississippi, compared to districts such as eastern Louisiana, where litigation is more frequent. Cases are simply not brought in some districts, notably those with low urban populations, because the motivation, skills, and facilities required to carry on litigation are lacking. The eastern Pennsylvania district with its large urban and industrial population presents an example

Amount of Litigation in Certain Districts   TABLE 4

District	Population in Thousands	Population in Thousands (Cities over 50,000)	Labor Cases	Civil Liberties
Southern Mississippi	1178	0	2	4
Northern Georgia	1722	487	6	7
Eastern Louisiana	1395	780	41	18
Eastern Pennsylvania	4743	2730	145	48

in which litigation occurs more frequently than in any of the Southern districts.

Although one may expect that Southern districts such as southern Mississippi would be a prolific source of civil liberties litigation, the absence of much litigation indicates the inactivity which the federal judiciary can exhibit in shaping policy in an area unless initiative is taken by interested participants. For all practical purposes, during our sample period, the federal district courts — and as a result much of the higher judiciary — were excluded from these districts by the failure of litigation to develop.

To test the effects of environmental differences, we isolated certain of our cases and observed their relation to an important social variable in the districts. Our group of cases included all race relations cases involving Negroes decided in the Southern district courts. We compared the results of the decisions with the size of the Negro population in the district. Since race relations cases deal with the most sensitive issue in Southern politics, we might expect decisions in the district courts to be related to Negro-white population balance. Other Southern behaviors are strongly related to this factor.

The overall correlation between the direction of decisions and the percentage of Negroes in the district is r = .42. (See Figure 1.) The modest but definite direction of correlation indicates that court policies are related to variations in racial population in the same manner as observed in other areas of Southern politics. A close relationship is most visible in districts with extreme population imbalance, either with or without Negroes. The districts of southern Georgia, northern Mississippi, and southern Mississippi all have large Negro populations and low scores in deciding cases for Negroes, whereas the districts of western Virginia, eastern Tennessee, and middle Tennessee have small Negro populations and high scores. In most other districts the relationship is not as pronounced, and in several, notably the northern district of Texas and the eastern district of Louisiana, the relationship is reversed. For example, the northern Texas district has few Negroes but a low civil rights score, and the eastern Louisiana district has a comparatively

Relationship of Percentage of Cases in District
Decided in Favor of Negroes in Race Relations Cases
to Percentage of Negro Population in That District   FIGURE 1

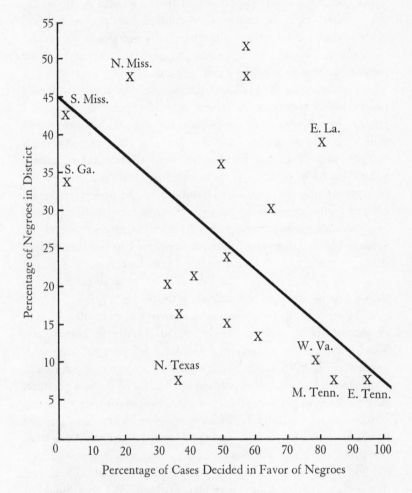

For the purpose of this analysis, we have broadened our coverage to include cases decided from 1957 to 1962 in eleven Southern districts with more than five cases.

Source: *Race Relations Law Reporter.*

large Negro population but decided a large proportion of cases favorably to Negroes.

Our evidence indicates that the correlation between race relations policy and Negro-white population balance is weaker in the Southern judiciary than in many other political institutions. Political science literature indicates that the relation is stronger in the actions of Southern officials in registering Negroes to vote and in the behavior of Southern legislators and governors.[11]

In accounting for these differences we note that Southern district judges, unlike most other Southern political officials, are appointed for life, are not removable for political reasons, and are not responsible to Southern public opinion in any formal ways. Although recruitment policies suggest that Southern district judges possess values similar in many respects to those of other Southerners, the life tenures and quasi-insulated positions of the federal judiciary prevent reinforcement of such values through activities like popular elections and public campaigning. In addition, district judges are subjected to pressures from national appellate courts to have their decisions conform to national policies. For these reasons it would seem that Southern judges are less affected by political pressures than are many other political officials in the South.

The district judge is required by statute to live in his district, and he participates as a person in the life of the district community. Thus, although federal judges are insulated from formal links with popular opinion, they are aware of opinions expressed in a community context, and such expression is a variety of popular pressure. A notable example is the case in the eastern district of South Carolina in which Judge J. Waties Waring struck down an attempt by the state to block Negro voting. This action effectively isolated him from the entire Charleston community, and it was said that old friends ignored him, acquaintances refused to speak to him, and that he became the "lonesomest man in town." [12] Other Southern

---

[11] See V. O. Key, *Southern Politics* (New York: Alfred A. Knopf, 1949) on Southern politics generally, and Donald R. Matthews and James W. Prothro, "Social and Economic Factors and Negro Voter Registration in the South," 67 *American Political Science Review* (1963), pp. 24–44, for the influence of Southern registrars.

[12] Samuel Grafton, "Lonesomest Man in Town," 125 *Colliers* (1950), pp.

judges suffered similar social indignities after decisions favorable to civil rights, among them Judge Skelly Wright of the Louisiana eastern district and Judge Frank Johnson of the middle district of Alabama. Graves of their relatives were desecrated, crosses burned on home lawns, dynamite blasts set off near relatives' homes, and professional ostracism was inflicted by local bar groups. When Judge Wright was slated for a promotional appointment to the Fifth Circuit Court of Appeals, a Louisiana Senator intervened to block the appointment. Wright was, however, later appointed to an appeals court in the District of Columbia.[13]

These incidents indicate that federal judges may function with a degree of independence. If a judge persists in the face of public harassment, he may still continue to be an effective decision maker — a striking and crucial contrast to legislators in the same position in the South. Judge Waring expressed his feeling for the judicial role in the following words:

> I'd never thought about the race problem, most of my life. . . . By being a judge I've gradually acquired a passion for justice. I'd never really met any Negroes, except as laborers. Then in the courtroom I began to see the realities and inequalities. It gives one a sense of futility at times. . . . I began to see illogicalities, and suddenly the whole segregation system appeared absurd.[14]

Although judges ordinarily adjudicate within their own districts, they do, on occasion, serve outside their locality. As a gross measure, for example, all district judges spent 1,926 days holding court outside their own circuit in 1960, an average of little more than a week per judge. This included service in other circuits for a variety of purposes, such as filling vacancies, helping out with heavy case loads, and substituting for judges temporarily out of service. The outside service does not appear to be a systematic plan to place judges outside their localities and delocalize them.

20–21 and 49–50. See also Jack Peltason, *Fifty-Eight Lonely Men* (New York: Harcourt, Brace and World, 1961).

[13] Joel Grossman, *Lawyers and Judges* (New York: John Wiley and Sons, 1965), p. 28, footnote 16.

[14] Grafton, "Lonesomest Man in Town," p. 49.

The intervention of an outside judge in a case can have important political consequences. An example is the activity of Judge Ronald N. Davies from the district of North Dakota in an important case in the Little Rock school desegregation controversy.[15] Judge Davies sat on temporary assignment to alleviate court work after the retirement of Judge Thomas Trimble and took a series of actions strongly supportive of desegregation in the schools. At a time when community pressures ran strongly against civil rights, this Eisenhower-appointed Republican from a non-Southern district decided critical cases and supported civil rights in Arkansas.

Patterns of Decision Making

In selecting labor and civil liberties cases, we have concentrated on important policy areas in which we would expect differences in political behavior among district judges to be quite visible. Examination of race relations cases in the districts has revealed behavioral differences among judges. Now we examine the entire group of cases. (See Table 5.)

Our sample of cases in the district courts identified 815 cases that were decided by individual judges; the remaining 76 were decided by three-judge courts and will be discussed later. We have observed the unequal distribution of cases among the circuits, but

Distribution of Cases Decided by District Judges and Number of Judges Deciding in Circuit   TABLE 5

| Cases | Third Circuit | | Fifth Circuit | | Eighth Circuit | |
Number of Cases	Number of Judges	Percentage of All Cases Decided	Number of Judges	Percentage of All Cases Decided	Number of Judges	Percentage of All Cases Decided
0–9	23	17.8	32	53.3	20	65.0
10–24	13	47.1	5	30.2	4	35.0
25 and over	5	35.1	1	16.5	0	0.0

[15] Peltason, *Fifty-Eight Lonely Men*, pp. 164–174.

also interesting is the variation in the amount of decision making among the judges themselves.

Clearly, district judges differed considerably in the number of cases they heard, and a relatively small group of judges handled a disproportionately large share of the litigation. In the Third Circuit, five of the forty-one judges participating handled more than one-third of the cases, whereas in the Fifth, six of the thirty-eight handled almost half of all the cases. Judge Skelly Wright in the eastern Louisiana district handled about one-sixth of all labor and civil liberties cases (forty cases), nearly twice as many as any other judge in the Fifth Circuit.

The distribution of cases indicates that policy is decided in two crucial areas — civil rights and labor relations — by a minority of district judges. Only to a limited extent does the nature of the district determine decision making distribution, for although certain districts provide more opportunity for district judges to decide significant cases, wide differences exist among judges within districts. In the eastern district of Louisiana, for example, Judge Wright decided five times as many cases as Judge Christenberry, and in the eastern district of Pennsylvania, Judge Gourley handled twice as many cases as did his colleague Judge Clary.

Ostensibly, the courts are passive instruments of policy because they may hear only those cases brought to them, and because judges have little direct control over the flow of cases. It is quite probable, however, that judges discourage or invite litigation by their expressed attitudes and by their past behavior. Judge Skelly Wright's record in favor of civil liberties cases, particularly race relations cases, undoubtedly encouraged litigation in his court. Litigants unable to secure favorable decisions elsewhere in Louisiana regarded the federal district court in New Orleans as a haven to which they might turn for favorable judgments on civil liberties problems.

In the past, it has been possible for judges to specialize in certain types of cases and to hear these cases because of the manner in which cases were assigned to judges in the court. Schedules describing the times and places judges were sitting made it possible to predict roughly which judges would hear cases scheduled at given times. Through a combination of activities of plaintiffs and the judges themselves, it was thus possible for judges to differentiate the kinds of cases heard. It seems likely that a judge like Judge Skelly Wright, whose predilection for civil liberties cases was known, might thus have heard a comparatively large number of those cases that came to his court in New Orleans. This in turn encouraged litigants to seek actions in the district court in New Orleans under the supposition that Judge Wright would hear the case. Recently, there has been a tendency to resort to random assignment, but it is doubtful that even this system eliminates the manipulation of the types of cases heard. The chief judge of the court controls the assignment of cases, and because the process of assignment is informally carried out, we cannot document what principles govern the distribution of cases.

Table 6 compares the decisions of district judges who decided more than five cases in each category according to political direction. A pro-civil liberties decision represented a vote in favor of the liberty claimed, and a pro-labor decision represented one made in favor of the group interests of labor.

Thirty-six judges in the three circuits decided over five cases in one of the areas, and twenty of the judges decided over five in both the labor and civil liberties categories. A dominant pattern in the distribution is the great range of decision scores. Only in civil liberties cases in the Third Circuit was there anything approaching a con-

*Number of District Judges Deciding Cases for
Labor and Civil Liberties by Circuit
and Level of Support*　　　TABLE 6

| | Number of Judges | | | | | |
Percentage of Cases	Third Circuit Civil Liberties	Labor	Fifth Circuit Civil Liberties	Labor	Eighth Circuit Civil Liberties	Labor
Below 10	7	0	3	0	0	0
10–33.3	3	3	0	0	2	2
33.4–50	0	7	2	2	1	1
51–66.7	0	5	2	2	2	0
Above 66.7	0	5	2	2	0	1

sensus on the issues that appeared in district litigation. Indeed, it is evident that considerable conflict and political difference exist among district court judges in handling important issues.

The lack of agreement in the districts may result from the solitary role of the district judge who is not exposed to the compromises and other political processes of a collegiate court. A district judge may not take into account the extent to which his decision squares with those of other district courts. On the other hand, appellate bodies may deliberately try to play down disagreements and reach united decisions that can be presented as an impressive consensus to bolster the prestige of a given decision.

The distribution of scores indicates that the behavioral pattern in the district judiciary reflects conflict and a variety of opinion. Although it is difficult to compare court levels due to differences in the manner in which decisions are made, there appears to be as great a disagreement in the district courts as in the appeals courts,[16] It is tempting to dismiss behavioral differences among district judges with the assertion that their scores are not comparable because each district judge decides a different group of cases. There are two objections to this cavil. First, although district judges do not sit on the same cases, they do sit on cases that are similar in basic political conflicts and situation. Major tendencies in both labor and civil liberties litigation determine the characteristic patterns of cases and set the underlying political tone. Second, it is highly improbable that judges would hear distinctly different groups of cases in the same area. For these reasons, we would argue, the scores indicating judicial behavior measure phenomena so similar that comparison of scores is possible.

Table 6 does not reveal the relationship between judges' disposition of labor and their disposition of civil liberties cases. To investigate the association for the twenty judges with scores in both categories, we compared the two groups of case scores by means of coefficients of correlation. The scores of ten judges in the district courts of the Third Circuit and seven judges in the Fifth were examined by this means; the Eighth Circuit contained too small a number to permit analysis.

[16] See Chapter Six.

The relationship between judges' disposition of labor and civil liberties cases was .24, a correlation indicating the association was not statistically significant (p. > .05). Although labor and civil liberties attitudes are often not closely associated in other social groups, for example in the working class, we might have expected a closer association on the part of district judges.

The scores of judges in the Fifth and Third Circuits were compared separately as a means of controlling for region. When this was done, very different results were obtained for judges in the two regions. The labor and civil liberties dispositions were correlated by an association of .55 in the Third Circuit, whereas the correlation was .26 for the judges in the Fifth Circuit. It seems that judges in the northern and eastern states of the Third Circuit decide cases fairly consistently in the two issue areas from an ideological point of view. Southern judges in the Fifth Circuit, on the other hand, produce a more complex attitudinal pattern in the disposition of cases. The reactions of Southern and Northern judges are similar to attitudes evinced by other politicians from the same two regions. Southern policy makers, because of regional problems, demonstrate complex patterns of liberalism and conservatism. Two Southern judges epitomized this complexity. Judge Skelly Wright from the eastern district of Louisiana had high scores in both the pro-civil liberties (62.5 per cent) and pro-labor (68.8 per cent) categories. Judge Joe M. Ingraham from the southern district of Texas scored a low 7.7 per cent for cases decided in favor of civil liberties, but he had a 55.6 per cent mark for deciding cases in favor of labor. Other Southern judges, although their behavior was not as extreme, sometimes decided both labor and civil liberties cases in favor of the liberal assumptions, but more often treated the two issue areas inconsistently.

Other studies have indicated that different behaviors among judges are related to party affiliation.[17] Our investigation of this relationship was conducted by determining the party identification of judges and then comparing the decisional scores of Republicans

[17] Stuart Nagel, "Political Party Affiliation and Judges' Decisions," 55 *American Political Science Review* (1961), pp. 843–851.

Relationship of Judges' Party and
Direction of Decisions (N = 33)   TABLE 7

Labor (349 cases)	Democrats more favorable than Republicans by 8.6 per cent
Civil Liberties (195 cases)	Republicans more favorable than Democrats by 13.3 per cent

and Democrats in each of the subject areas of our investigation. Party membership was related to disposition of cases according to Table 7.

In Table 7, party is shown to be slightly related to disposition of cases for both labor and civil liberties. The more favorable labor scores of the Democratic judges parallel the Democrats' tendency in national politics to favor labor interests. The difference is not, however, as great as has been found in studies of national party leaders or national legislators. Individual Democratic judges such as Judge Wallace Gourley of the middle district of Pennsylvania and Judge Skelly Wright of Louisiana had high labor scores but their performance was balanced by the anti-labor postures of conservative Southern Democrats. On the other hand, a contrast in party positions is provided by the performances of Judge Gourley and Judge Francis Van Dusen, a Republican also sitting in Pennsylvania. Each decided 33 labor cases during the time examined, but Judge Gourley favored labor 81.9 per cent of the time, whereas Judge Van Dusen did so in only 45.5 per cent of the cases.

The somewhat more favorable decisions of Republican judges on civil rights reflect ambiguity within each party on the subject, particularly among the Democrats. In the South, Eisenhower appointees such as Judge Frank Johnson of the middle Alabama district evinced a more favorable attitude toward civil rights than many Southern Democrats on the bench, and some Democrats in the North such as Judge Gourley had more favorable civil liberties records than Republicans. In addition, studies of party and ideology elsewhere have shown that differences between Republicans and Democrats on civil liberties issues are somewhat blurred.

Influence of Opinions

All opinions delivered in the district courts are signed and, except for routine orders, vary greatly in length. In contrast, decisions in European courts have demonstrated that a body of law can be built up by very short and unsigned opinions.

One public law scholar, Oliver Field, has speculated on why opinions accompanying decisions in American courts are usually published, explicitly signed, and of such length.[18] He discovered primarily legalistic reasons related to the development of the common law and the necessity for clarifying precedents. There are also important political reasons why American courts accompany decisions by elaborate opinions. For one thing, a tradition that developed in early American politics dictates that courts and legislators alike have a duty to make the law and the reasons underlying it known. Such traditions are consistent with the theory that court institutions should be subject to popular control. Lengthy opinions, the publication of these opinions, and the explicit signing of majority and dissenting opinions are all practices that potentially link the courts to more democratic responsibility.

A defense of popular control over the district courts was stated by a district judge in his dissent to a three-judge court opinion:

> It is the universal conviction of the people of the South also that the judges who function in the circuit should render justice in individual cases against a background of, and as interpreters of, the ethos of the people whose servants they are.[19]

Mississippi Judge Sidney Mize's statement above could hardly be a clearer call for popular control over the local federal courts, for it explicitly supports the primacy of public opinion and local values in court decisions. Other district judges have also justified decisions cit-

[18] Oliver Peter Field, *Judicial Review of Legislation in Ten Selected States* (Bloomington: Bureau of Government Research of Indiana University, 1937), pp. 58–69.

[19] *Bowman* v. *Birmingham Transit Co.* 292 F. 2d., pp. 28–29 advance sheets and repeated in *Wood* v. *United States* 295 F. 2d. 292 ff. We are indebted to Professor Joel Grossman for calling our attention to this passage.

ing the political climate of local public opinion.[20] Such citations are made particularly frequently by Southern judges in cases which deal with the implementation of racial equality.

On occasion, opinions delivered from the district bench are reminiscent of the racial demagoguery of Southern state leaders. A particularly notorious opinion was delivered by Judge Whitfield Davidson of the northern Texas district on the desegregation of the Dallas schools. Main headings of the opinion included "THE TRAGIC ERA," "RACIAL INTEGRITY IN HISTORY," "INTEGRATION OF RACES BY FORCE," and "HOME RULE — THAT BOON OF LOCAL SELF GOVERNMENT," and included oratory such as this in the eighteen-page opinion:

> In Haiti the integration had been but shortly allowed when one race destroyed the other. In Puerto Rico integration and amalgamation early became the order. In the Southern States the white and the former slave each retained his racial integrity. Is the Puerto Rican any better advanced than the Southern Negro? No Southern Negro has ever shot up the halls of Congress, killed the President's bodyguard and sought his life. One was integrated and the other was not.[21]

Even when upholding Negro rights, Southern judges often comment on the character of Negro activity as in the opinion by Louisiana's Judge Ben Dawkins deploring Negro bloc voting:

> We deplore the Negro practice of "bloc voting" with which all observant persons are familiar. . . . It is to be earnestly hoped that in the future those Negroes who are qualified to vote will achieve a degree of political maturity so as to vote according to the best interest of their State and Nation rather than for their own selfish or venal purposes.[22]

Although many Southern judges support Southern racial segregation in their opinions, an occasional judge defends political equality and national values. The most vigorous voice expressing those senti-

[20] See Robert Steamer, "The Role of the Federal District Courts in the Segregation Controversy," 22 *Journal of Politics* (1960), pp. 417–438.

[21] *Borders* v. *Rippy* 184 F. Supp. 402 (1960).

[22] *U.S.* v. *Association of Citizens' Councils of America* 196 F. Supp. 911 (1961).

ments in the district courts was Judge Skelly Wright, who once commented in a school desegregation case:

> The problems attendant to desegregation in the deep South are considerably more serious than generally appreciated in some sections of our country. The problem of changing a people's mores, particularly those with an emotional overlay, is not to be taken lightly. It is a problem which will require the utmost patience, understanding, generosity and forbearance for all of us, whatever race. But the magnitude of the problem may not nullify the principle. And that principle is that we are, all of us, freeborn Americans, with a right to make our way, unfettered by sanctions imposed by man because of the work of God.[23]

None of the expressions cited above was necessary to the decision of the case at hand. They were, rather, reports to constituencies and public statements of judicial values. In tone they often invoked the styles and feelings that were expressed by nonjudicial politicians, putting judges' positions on the record and establishing links with local public opinion. Independently situated and life-tenured, district judges do not need to mend fences in this manner to retain political office, and rarely aspire to other political office once appointed to the federal bench. The reasons for these expressive opinions are suggested in previous chapters, which have dealt with the local character of judicial constituencies, the effect of local factors on recruitment, and the lack of national control and integration in the federal judiciary.

Impact of the Legal Subculture

Decision making in the district courts is shaped, as we have seen, by strong local democratic features. So strong and visible has been the influence of local values in the districts that litigants have requested judges to be disqualified in local cases, and a leading law journal has published an article on the problems raised by such judicial behavior and on ways by which district judges might be disciplined.[24]

The eighty-eight district courts are united, however, by certain

[23] *Bush* v. *Orleans Parish School Board* 138 F. Supp. 341–342 (1960).
[24] "Judicial Performance in the Fifth Circuit," 73 *Yale Law Journal* (1963), pp. 90–133.

legal considerations that give uniformity to their decisions and institutional behavior, at the same time that the centrifugal forces of localism are at work. An important experience that pulls judges together is their socialization in legal education. Since most judges have read the same or similar hornbooks, taken similar courses of instruction, and been exposed to many common values in law school, legal education brings some common perspective to decision making. In bar organizations and in further readings in the law, the common elements of legal culture are further disseminated to judges.

The judicial process also provides procedures by which differences among the district courts are refined and common values inculcated into judicial decision making. Since any district decision can be heard in the courts of appeals and may be heard by the Supreme Court, both the regional appellate courts and the Supreme Court can supply uniform standards through review of district court decisions and by remand and vacate order. But it is a mistake to believe that orders and decisions in appellate review are rigidly followed by the local district courts.[25] Indeed, an important political feature of the judicial process is the promptness and the extent to which lower courts observe the directives in appellate decisions. The idea that either the Supreme Court or the appeals courts adequately supervises the district courts is not empirically supportable but, in general, higher court review of district decisions is a cohesive force.

Another important factor unifying the district courts has been their adherence to common legal concepts and rules of procedure. At the beginning of the American court system, the judiciary act passed in 1789 allowed a great deal of local autonomy in legal procedures, providing that actions in district courts were the same in each state "as are now used or allowed in the supreme courts of the same."[26] The general rule of conformity to state practices had many exceptions, and federal procedure dominated in such im-

[25] See, for example, Walter Murphy, "Lower Court Checks on Supreme Court Power," 53 *American Political Science Review* (1959), pp. 1017–1031, and Kenneth Vines, "The Role of Circuit Courts of Appeals in the Federal Judicial Process: A Case Study," 7 *Midwest Journal of Political Science* (1963), pp. 314–316.

[26] Wright, *Federal Courts,* p. 220.

portant matters as the administration of the trial, appellate procedure, and questions of jurisdiction. Conflicting decisions on whether state or federal procedures were more important in the district courts resulted, but the individual judge was ordinarily able to emphasize the procedures of his choice.

It was not until 1938 that Congress, under the urging of legal groups, passed a uniform Code of Civil Procedure, which embodied rules and procedures governing conduct throughout the federal court system. This was followed in 1946 by the passage of a Federal Rules of Criminal Procedure, which provided uniform practices for noncivil cases.[27] The codes were a significant step in providing legal integration of the federal court system, and their success in providing procedural uniformity has been called "quite phenomenal" by one authority.[28] The acceptance of the codes also enhanced the power of legal groups to make the rules under which the courts operate. Although the basic legislation was enacted by the Congress, the rules were originally drafted by a committee consisting of the leading lawyers and law professors in the country and were then submitted to the Supreme Court for revision. When the Congress passed no adverse legislation after submission, the rules as drafted became law.[29] The adoption of the codes was an impressive demonstration of the power of legal groups to enact important modifications of federal judicial institutions.

Judicial conferences and councils, instigated by Chief Justice Taft and urged by legal groups, have provided a further means of unifying the district courts. At the present time federal judges meet in the following organizations:

(1) Judicial Conference of the United States, where the Chief Justice presides over a group consisting of the chief judge of each circuit, the chief judge of the Court of Claims, and a district judge chosen from each circuit.

(2) Judicial Conference of the Circuit, in which the chief judge

---

27 *Ibid.*, pp. 220–225.
28 *Ibid.*, p. 225.
29 *Ibid.*

of each circuit presides over the annual meeting of the appeals and district judges of the circuit.

(3) Judicial Council, a twice yearly meeting of appeals judges of a circuit presided over by the chief judge.[30]

The Judicial Conference was initially created by the act of 1922, which grew out of enthusiasm for improving the administration of the courts. Heated controversy in the Congress marked the debate over the assignability of judges provision. The power of the conference to shift judges from one district to another according to need was seen by many congressmen as destroying the principle of localism in federal court institutions.[31] Although the provision was passed, it has been used only modestly to meet court needs, and its political effects are rarely discernible. The provision that the councils were to recommend personnel changes and make other suggestions relating to administration also increased the power of the legal order. As we have seen, the councils are influential in deciding what positions shall be added to the federal judiciary, although they have not intruded into the appointment process. Recommendations and provisions for modifying legal procedures are also one of the duties of the councils, and they have been influential in spreading such practices as pre-trial conferences.

The most important supervisory function exercised has been the national circulation of judges through the assignability practice. Recommendations regarding administration of the courts, although important, have not added materially to the nationalization of the judiciary. Neither have effective disciplinary practices been established for overseeing the judiciary. In an exceptional action, a judicial council disciplined a federal district judge accused of malpractice by enjoining him from conducting further judicial business after completing the current docket. Doubts were publicly ex-

[30] For the structure of the judicial conferences and councils, see *Field Study of the Operations of United States Courts,* Report to Senate Appropriations Committee, April 1959. On their history see Felix Frankfurter and James Landis, *The Business of the Supreme Court* (New York: Macmillan, 1927), pp. 230–254.

[31] Frankfurter and Landis, *Business of the Supreme Court,* pp. 238–239.

pressed, however, as to whether the council has such powers.[32]

The supervisory functions of the judicial councils have established limited order and integration among the district courts. But the councils' greatest importance has been the creation of occasions for group meetings in which the district judge participates in a larger regional and national context than his accustomed local district.

[32] *The New York Times,* December 29, 1965, p. 14.

DECISION MAKING IN
THE COURTS OF APPEALS

The United States courts of appeals occupy a crucial position in the federal judicial system because of the finality of their decisions and the character of their activities. Created to relieve the Supreme Court and to make possible the extension of federal jurisdiction, the appeals courts have grown into "courts of last resort in the run of ordinary cases." [1] Thus, nine out of ten cases heard in the courts of appeals are not heard again, and 95 per cent of all federal litigation begun in the district courts ends without review by the Supreme Court. [2]

[1] *Textile Mills Securities Corporation* v. *Commissioner of Internal Revenue* 314 U.S. 326 (1941).
[2] Based on litigation filed. See *Annual Report of the Director of Administrative Office of the United States Courts,* 1960–1965.

CHAPTER SIX

Although district court decisions spring from numerous and undifferentiated types of litigation, cases arriving in the appeals courts have undergone initial screening and decision making activity. With rare exceptions, every case in the United States Courts of Appeals is an attempt to undo a previous judicial or administrative determination. As review agencies, therefore, the appeals courts represent a different stage in the decision making process and, for that reason, deal with somewhat different questions than those decided in the district courts. These considerations suggest that the institutional features of decision making in the appeals courts are different from those of the district courts and the Supreme Court.

Cases Filed: The Raw Materials
of Decision Making

Over the last ten years, cases filed in the courts of appeals have shown substantial increase. For example, in 1960, 3,899 cases were filed. By 1963 this number had increased to 5,437 cases, an increase of 13 per cent over the previous year.[3] In some circuits the average is far higher. The District of Columbia Circuit and the Fifth Circuit have had 20 per cent increases in some years. The expanded judicial business in the courts of appeals results from an increase in appeals from both district courts and administrative agencies.

The increased filings are of concern to the judiciary because, in the first place, there are only eleven circuits and less than a hundred appellate judges. Second, as we shall see later, decision making in the appeals court involves the time of three judges for every case normally heard by one judge in the district. Finally, an appellate docket is usually composed of more enduring sources of litigation and probably represents more complex issues than district courts. Cases have undergone one trial, have emerged in an initial decision, and would appear to represent issues of some importance.

Access to the Courts

Even though appealing a case requires additional expenditures of resources and continuing motivation by the litigants, the number of appealed cases is large. This is partially a result of the character of appellate jurisdiction, which makes access to the appellate courts relatively uninhibited. Appellate courts must review other institutional decisions. If a case meets jurisdictional requirements for access to the initial hearing, it is certain to meet them for appellate review. Primarily, the district courts establish the character of the appellate docket, because of the jurisdictional prerequisites necessary for entering the system at the district level. Thus, it should be emphasized that the work load of the courts of appeals is determined to a great degree by the scope of original jurisdiction given to the

[3] *Annual Report,* 1963, p. 188. Figures on litigation commenced.

district courts. If procedural requirements are met, a right of appeal is available. From the district courts come appeals arising under the Constitution, laws or treaties of the United States, civil actions between citizens of different states, offenses against a law of the United States, and other areas covered by statutes.[4] Actually, an average of less than 4 per cent of cases begun in the district courts seeks access to the appellate courts.[5] However, as shown in Table 1, cases appealed from district courts are increasing.[6]

Access to Appeals Courts: Cases Filed
in 1960 and 1963   TABLE 1

Source	1960	1963
United States district courts	3,077	4,193
Boards and commissions	737	1,141
Original proceedings	67	99
Other	18	4
Totals	3,899	5,437

Source: *Annual Report of the Director of Administrative Office of the United States Courts*, 1960, 1963.

Administrative agencies are the other major source of appellate litigation. Under a variety of statutes, right of appeal to the "regular" court system is available for litigants who receive judgments from independent regulatory agencies and commissions. This avenue of access continues to expand mainly because of the growth of administrative agencies' activities and the increasingly significant questions brought before them for initial adjudication.

Finally, a small portion of the courts of appeals docket is original jurisdiction by writs of mandamus and prohibition.[7] While other

[4] *United States Code*, 28:1331, 1332.
[5] Based on litigation filed. See *Annual Report*, for ten year average.
[6] See *United States Code*, 28:1291 for administrative agency reviews, and *Annual Report*, 1963, p. 188, for district appeals.
[7] Charles Bunn, *A Brief Survey of the Jurisdiction and Practice of the Courts of the United States* (St. Paul: West Publishing Co., 1949), p. 199.

routes are important, it is clear that access to the courts of appeal is primarily through the avenue of the district courts.

Varieties of Appeals

Although the business of the courts of appeals is large, it is not composed of cases of uniform significance. The fact that a case is appealed cannot always be equated with importance, since a large portion of the business of the appellate courts does not involve major policy issues in society.

Among the types of appeals considered by the courts of appeals are:

(1) *Ritualistic appeals*. The demands and expectations of a constituency often require an appeal to be made from a district decision, even when it is obvious that there is no chance for reversal. Appealing one's case "all the way to the Supreme Court" suggests the commitment to a cause that is expected of public representatives in certain kinds of litigation. Even when directions from the Supreme Court are specific and the attitude of the court of appeals clear, such cases are appealed, only to be turned down on review. Such ritualistic appeals are frequent in civil·rights litigation and were a common pattern of behavior in the school desegregation decisions in the Fifth Circuit. The appellate courts often answer such appeals quickly, but sometimes the ritualistic appeal provides the opportunity for judges in the minority on the appellate courts to express dissatisfaction with the circuit's current stance on the issue under review. The ritualistic appeal should not be dismissed as having no political importance, since it does provide an opportunity for the defeated interests to shift the burden for the defeat outside the district and to assure their clienteles that they have done all within the rule of law that is possible to defend their interests.

(2) *Frivolous appeals*. Out of America's prisons comes a flood of appeals that can be categorized as "frivolous" — cases and claims which have no substance and little chance for success. Since a claim is occasionally successful, prisoners are motivated to try all kinds of devices to escape their sentences. Among the frivolous

appeals are most of the requests for *habeas corpus* and the demands that the court review a case in the face of new evidence.

(3) *Bureaucratic appeals.* Because of constitutional requirements for procedural due process, appeals from administrative agency decisions constitute a part of the appellate docket. Although reversal is infrequent, modification of administrative decisions is not. Some of these cases provide substantive policy issues for the society, and many involve major litigants — labor, industry, transportation, communications.

(4) *Consensual appeals.* This category of cases includes those in which there is substantial consensus in the courts as to how the issues should be resolved, even though individuals who have lost freedom or property hope to change the original verdict. These appeals are the "bread and butter" issues of the appellate docket, in which litigants continually seek modifications of lower court awards. Eminent domain, income tax cases, and corporate activity are often included in this category of cases.

(5) *Nonconsensual appeals.* A final category of appellate business includes the cases which raise major questions of public policy and upon which there is considerable disagreement. Here the decisions of the appellate courts affect not only the particular litigants under review, but establish policy for the society at large. Litigation in civil liberties, reapportionment, election disputes, religion, and education presents controversial questions of importance for all of society.

Screening the Docket

The rapidly increasing business of the district courts is reflected in the growing number of appeals. As is the case in the district courts, the appellate calendar is congested and delay is experienced in the processing of appeals cases. However, methods are available by which the court can exercise control over its docket, and important cases are, in most instances, decided expeditiously.

Although appellate litigation varies in length, the proceedings are generally less time-consuming than trials in the district courts.

Arguments are limited, briefs are presented and read in advance, and the process of review is less protracted than the process of original trial. In addition, a substantial portion of the cases filed is screened out without full hearing, as shown in Table 2.

Nature and Disposition of Courts
of Appeals Docket   TABLE 2

All Circuits	Cases Disposed By Consolidation Per Cent	N	Cases Disposed Without Hearing Per Cent	N	Cases Disposed After Hearing Per Cent	N	Total Cases
Criminal	8.6	(74)	23.5	(202)	67.9	(586)	(862)
U.S. civil	6.7	(69)	31.3	(328)	62.2	(652)	(1,049)
Private civil	6.8	(128)	23.1	(446)	69.7	(1,320)	(1,894)
Bankruptcy	5.4	(7)	20.8	(27)	73.8	(96)	(130)
Administrative appeals	1.2	(112)	41.2	(407)	46.0	(443)	(962)
Original proceedings	7.3	(8)	27.3	(30)	65.5	(72)	(110)
All others	0.0	(0)	25.0	(1)	75.0	(3)	(4)
Totals		(398)		(1,441)		(3,172)	5,011

Source: *Annual Report of the Director of Administrative Office of the United States Courts,* 1963.

A portion of the docket is reduced by consolidating similar claims into single cases. Not only does consolidation enable the circuit to reduce its work load, but equally important, it ensures that a common decision will emerge from the circuit over a group of common appeals. The major screening is achieved by the disposition of cases without hearing. The large number of filed cases effectively disposed of in this fashion includes those withdrawn by litigants and those which do not meet procedural requirements.

Through screening by consolidation and pre-hearing disposition, the courts of appeals reduce the cases filed to a selected body of litigation for full review. Even here, as will be noted later, oral decisions and *per curiam* decisions provide avenues by which the courts can quickly dispose of their responsibilities.

Institutional Character of Decision Making

For those cases not disposed of by screening methods prior to a full review, briefs are filed and oral arguments are heard, usually by a court of appeals panel of three judges. In cases subject to quick settlement, a *per curiam* opinion of a few sentences is written and a decision rendered without detailed opinion. About 25 per cent of all cases are *per curiam* decisions.[8] On rare occasions, judges settle a case by rendering an opinion orally from the bench, but only in those instances in which lower court opinion is affirmed without modification.

For those cases not disposed of before the hearing, or by *per curiam* or oral opinion, a conference is held following the week of the argument. Opinions are prepared, read by individual judges, and discussed, and writing the majority opinion is assigned by the presiding judge. Because the screening methods greatly reduce the appellate docket, the actual number of cases terminated by individual circuit judges is modest, as shown in Table 3.

Average of Circuit Cases Terminated per Judge in 1963   TABLE 3

Circuit	Number of Judges	Case Load per Judge
First	3	48
Second	9	77
Third	8	48
Fourth	5	73
Fifth	9	86
Sixth	6	63
Seventh	7	60
Eighth	7	38
Ninth	9	65
Tenth	6	55
District of Columbia	9	74

Source: *Annual Report of the Director of Administrative Office of the United States Courts,* 1963.

[8] *Annual Report,* 1963.

Perhaps the most important institutional feature of appellate decision making is its collegial nature, a practice recognized by statute in the 1948 revisions of the judicial code.[9] The individual appeals courts are authorized to hear cases in separate panels of three judges, assignments to such panels being made as the court directs. Only two circuits specifically provide for making the assignment in their rules, but, except for the District of Columbia, circuit panel assignments are made by the chief judge of the circuit or by a judge designated by him.[10] Since all but one of the eleven circuits have more than three judges, a circuit court membership is divided into three-member committees to hear cases, sometimes in various cities throughout the area. Thus, several circuit cases can be heard simultaneously by different groups of three justices each.

The political consequences of this committee operation of appellate decision making are substantial. First, the political composition of the entire court's membership indicates less about the circuit's behavior than is the case at the Supreme Court level. Six liberal and three conservative appointees on an appeals court may suggest to liberal interests in society that all is well at the appellate level. Thus, we hear a great deal about which interests have a "majority" on the circuit court. This assumes, however, that appellate decisions are majoritarian decisions of the entire membership; they are not. One cannot transfer to the circuit courts the organizational or behavioral patterns of the Supreme Court. The panel composition of decision making means that a majority domination is probable, but not certain, depending upon the make-up of the individual panel. For if two conservative judges appear on a panel, it makes no difference how many liberal judges are in the circuit if the decision of the two conservative judges is not challenged in re-hearing.

A second consequence of the panel system is that it throws into different perspective the relationship between the circuits and the

9 *United States Code*, 28:46a.

10 See Delmar Karlen, *Appellate Courts in the United States and England* (New York: New York University Press, 1963), Chap. 4, and Louis Loeb, "Judicial Blocs and Judicial Values in Four Selected United States Courts of Appeals 1957–1960 Terms" (unpublished Ph.D. dissertation, American University, 1964), p. 39.

Supreme Court. The higher court rarely confirms or reverses decisions made by the entire circuit membership. It relates, by and large, to circuit panels. Thus, a high rate of reversal for a circuit may reveal that a majority of the appellate court is in opposition to the Supreme Court. It may also suggest, however, that judges of the minority position on the appellate court are reversed simply because they are adjudicating together in a particular case. Their view may not represent the aggregate position of the circuit at all. To say that the Supreme Court reversed a particular circuit fewer times than another circuit is not what it appears to mean.

A third effect of the panel system is that it enhances the opportunity for intracourt conflicts on policy positions. Efforts to find agreement on policy within a circuit are an important factor in appellate behavior. But when two sets of judges are hearing similar cases in the same circuit, there is no guarantee that uniformity will emerge.

The panel system also reduces the opportunity for dissent within each case. As will be noted later, dissenting opinions are infrequent in circuit cases. A partial explanation for the difference in dissent behavior between the circuits and the Supreme Court is simply that groups of three are less likely to be in conflict than groups of nine.

Finally, the three-judge committee system and the practice by which these panels are selected in most circuits give to the chief judge of the circuit a considerable amount of power. The chief judge, the senior judge in length of service under the age of seventy, is administrative head of the circuit. In most circuits, he selects the panels and also assigns retired circuit judges (senior judges) to active duty to relieve congested dockets. By structuring the panels according to his preference, he can influence the outcome of decisions. As in the committee system of the United States Senate, the chief judge holds his position exclusively on the basis of his length of service, and thus he may or may not reflect the majority judicial stance in his circuit. In contrast with the chief justice of the United States, the chief judge is not appointed to his position of power, but moves toward it by tenure, regardless of the political climate of the national government. His power of assignment, coupled with his power to activate senior judges, gives to the chief judge a potentially enormous influence over the disposition of the docket.

In an effort to compensate for the consequences of the committee panel system of the appellate courts, the *en banc* procedure was established to resolve intracircuit conflicts.[11] This procedure permits, either upon application by the litigants or by judges of the court, an opportunity for all of the judges in the circuit to sit together on critical policy questions or cases in which intracircuit conflict exists. The Uniform Rules for Appellate Procedure prescribe that an *en banc* hearing "is not favored" and should only be granted when (1) consideration by the full court is necessary to secure or maintain uniformity of its decisions, and (2) when the proceeding involves a question of exceptional importance.

The *en banc* process is relatively new in the appellate courts; it was first recognized by the Supreme Court in 1941 when it was resolving a dispute between judges of the Third and Ninth Circuits.[12] Although the procedure received statutory sanction in the Judicial Code of 1948, the circuits still have discretion to decide if and how it will be utilized, and, as a result, a great variety in its use has developed in the circuits. Its use, though small, is growing. Between 1954 and 1964 the number of cases heard *en banc* tripled so that, during 1964, the courts of appeals heard fifty-one cases *en banc* or about 1.5 per cent of all cases decided.

The type of intracircuit conflict that *en banc* was designed to resolve can be seen in the cases of *Mottolese* v. *Kaufman* and *Beiersdorf and Company* v. *McGohey* in the Second Circuit.[13] In the first case, Judges Hand, Frank, and Swan constituted the panel, which was asked to issue a writ of mandamus ordering a federal district judge to proceed with a trial without waiting until a state court had acted. Hand and Swan voted to deny the petition and Frank dissented, arguing that the district judge's stay was an abuse of his

[11] Judah L. Labovitz, "En Banc Procedures on the Federal Courts of Appeals," 111 *University of Pennsylvania Law Review* (1962), p. 220.

[12] *Textile Mills Security Corp.* v. *Commissioner* 314 U.S. 326 (1941).

[13] *Mottolese* v. *Kaufman* 176 F. 2d. 301 (1949) and *Beiersdorf and Company* v. *McGohey* 187 F. 2d. 14 (1951).

discretion. Two years later the same question came up again in the *Beiersdorf* case, and Frank was on a panel with Justices Clark and Chase. Frank found a new ally for his views in Justice Clark, and the minority position he had held in the first case became the majority position in the second. Thus, two different holdings had emerged on the question from the Second Circuit simply because of a shift in panels and a new interpersonal alliance pattern.

Although *en banc* was designed as an instrument of conflict resolution, it appears to have developed into an institutionalization of conflict. *En banc* does not seem to resolve intracircuit conflict, but reveals it in a formalized setting. In some circuits, four out of five *en banc* cases include at least one dissenting opinion, and in two out of five cases the majority decision is by only one vote.[14] Because of frequent disputes in *en banc* cases, such decisions are often ignored by minority members of the court in their subsequent panel deliberations.[15] If the *en banc* process often does not resolve intraconflict differences, what then are its political consequences?

A major utilization of the *en banc* process is in cases in which disciplinary action or restraint is requested for judicial personnel. Such cases include requesting a judge of a district court to excuse himself from a case after he refused to do so, vacating judgments of district judges who were improperly seated, issuing writs because district judges have abused their discretion, intimidation of jurors, and improper conduct by an officer of the courts. In these instances, the *en banc* procedure becomes a specialized trial over the behavior of one of its members and constitutes a disciplinary review board.

Another use of *en banc* occurs in the circuits when they wish to use the authority of the full court in order to improve the chances for a decision's acceptance. This was especially true in the Fourth and Fifth Circuits in civil rights litigation. The circuits desired that a full and, if possible, unanimous court would determine the major cases in an effort to ensure compliance. In this respect the *en banc*

[14] A. Lamar Alexander, Jr., "En Banc Hearings in the Federal Courts of Appeals: Accommodating Institutional Responsibilities," 40 *New York University Law Review* (1965), p. 583.

[15] *Ibid.*, p. 584.

procedure resembles the efforts of the Supreme Court to obtain a unanimous decision in *Brown* v. *Board of Education*.

The *en banc* process is also directed toward the Supreme Court. There is a feeling, substantiated in part by reversal patterns, that the Supreme Court is less likely to reverse an *en banc* decision than a panel decision in the circuit.[16] Appearing before the Supreme Court as a united circuit, or at least in a case in which the entire circuit has participated, is an effective pressure against review and reversal. The politics of intersystem behavior place great value on support from the high court, and *en banc* is seen as a device that enhances this support.

It is true that *en banc* cannot be considered more than a partial counteraction to the decisive effects of the panel system. However, the procedure does provide a more complete picture of conflict and consensus within the court, making analysis of intracircuit judicial behavior possible.

The Character of Appellate Decision Making

Decision making in the courts of appeals covers not only issues and litigants but also decisions made earlier in district courts or administrative agencies. It is therefore intrinsically "relational behavior," composed of responses to other decision makers. It is also relational in that the collegial nature of the appellate courts requires interaction within the court when formulating a decision. Thus, appellate decision making is a web of collegial responses to other institutions, the political character of which is determined by the nature and direction of these responses.

Decision making in the appeals courts can be investigated by inspecting two non-consensus areas of litigation, civil liberties and labor cases, in the Third, Fifth, and Eighth Circuits for the period 1956 to 1961.[17] This allows comparisons with a similar sample in the

[16] See reversal and support patterns of Supreme Court in its review of *en banc* cases, *ibid.,* pp. 746–749.

[17] A "civil liberties" case is one in which a claim is made under the Bill of Rights, Thirteenth, Fourteenth, or Fifteenth Amendments, or Article I, Section 9, of the Constitution. For a modified use of this standard, see S. Sidney Ulmer, "Supreme Court Behavior and Civil Rights," 13 *Western*

district courts and investigation of litigation in which substantial policy differences are likely to exist. Table 4 indicates the civil liberties and labor docket of the three sample circuits between 1956 and 1961.

Civil Liberties and Labor Cases
        on Appeal 1956–1961   TABLE 4

Circuit	Labor Cases	Civil Liberties
Third	157	120
Fifth	293	391
Eighth	67	138
Totals	517	649

Source: Sample of cases.

Appellate Transformation of Cases

A striking feature of the appellate court docket is the enlargement of the civil liberties policy functions at the circuit level. This enlargement arises largely from cases which did not deal with civil liberties in the district courts. Of the 649 civil liberties cases on appeal, only 217 involved civil liberties litigation in the district courts. These data indicate that one of the important political functions of the appellate process in the federal courts is the transformation of cases that were routine trial types in the district into cases with greater political significance as civil liberties issues. Obviously, the circuit courts do not actively seek such transformations, for they may hear only those cases appealed to them, in the form and with the issues that are raised by the litigants. However, the circuit courts do provide the environment and also the structure which makes the metamorphosis possible.

The development of district trial cases into civil liberties cases in the circuit courts may be illustrated by two examples. In *Reyes* v.

Political Quarterly (1960), p. 288. The terms "libertarian" and "non-libertarian" are used to distinguish judges and courts who hold for and against the civil liberty being claimed.

United States,[18] the defendant was convicted of a narcotics violation in the district court and the judge sentenced him to less than the minimum term provided under the law. Three days later, upon learning of his error, the district judge had the defendant brought into the court and increased the sentence. The defendant then appealed to the circuit court on the grounds that his constitutional rights had been violated. In a second case, *Proffer* v. *United States,*[19] the defendant was convicted in the district court of mail fraud and false and fraudulent misrepresentation in selling stocks. The defendant, who was a lawyer, had waived right to counsel. But upon conviction he appealed to the circuit court, claiming that his constitutional right of counsel during trial had been violated. As it happened, neither appeal to the circuit courts was successful. Both cases do exemplify, however, the process by which trials in the district courts, often having no formal written opinion, may upon the initiative of litigants become civil liberties cases in the circuit courts. Here they are heard by a collegial court, bring forth a formally written opinion, and sometimes evoke important policy decisions.

Like the two cases described above, the district court antecedents of our sample of circuit civil liberties cases frequently had no civil liberties character in the district courts. In their district court form they evidenced little policy salience but functioned as routinized federal trials of little individual political impact. Because of their lack of policy salience and interest, such cases often do not evoke written opinions from the judges that become part of the corpus of law.

At the time of their foundation in the Judiciary Act of 1891, the intermediate appellate courts were hardly intended to perform the functions our data reveal.[20] Created originally to shoulder the appellate burden for the Supreme Court and to make it possible for that court to deal more selectively and more deliberately with appellate work, the circuit courts have also provided the seedbed

---

[18] *Reyes* v. *United States,* 262 F. 2d. 801 (1959).

[19] *Proffer* v. *United States,* 288 F. 2d. 182 (1961).

[20] *Act of March 3, 1891,* was the first successful effort to create a separate level of intermediate appellate courts after the brief success in *Act of February 13, 1801.* Opposition was not based upon an anticipation of the court's transforming role. See Chapter Two of this study.

where numerous important policy cases are begun and often finally decided. The circuit courts, far from simply refining and echoing the work of the district courts, have, in effect, developed into courts of first instance for large numbers of civil liberties cases. Though placed in an intermediate position in the appellate process, they both initiate and conclude many policy questions in federal litigation. Their in-between location in the judicial system belies actual functions.

To assume, therefore, that the appellate process is largely a "filtering" operation and to base political analysis upon this assumption are inadequate. That fewer cases are heard at each higher level of the judiciary indicates that in terms of numbers alone, filtering does take place. But what escapes the formal notion of the appellate process is that the cases which are appealed are often radically different in their second hearing than in their first. Often the substance of the case shifts on appeal, and although the litigants remain the same, the judicial system permits a case to undergo significant transformation as it moves within the appellate process.

Relation of Appellate Decision Making to Other Decisions

Both in transformed cases and in those in which the appealed plea is unchanged, the courts of appeals abrogate a considerable number of former decisions. It is clear from Table 5 that appellate decision making affects various policy areas differently, substantially changing previous decisions in some areas more often than in others. Too, there is marked variation in the response of the three circuits.

Reversals of Civil Liberties and Labor Cases   TABLE 5

Circuit	Percentage Civil Liberties	Percentage Labor
Third	27.5 (33 of 120)	19.1 (30 of 157)
Fifth	29.7 (116 of 391)	33.8 (99 of 293)
Eighth	21.0 (29 of 138)	26.9 (18 of 67)

Source: Sample of cases.

The reversal activity of the appellate courts clearly shows that appealing a case is not always a legal ritual, but an act which often results in major modifications of earlier decisions. In this manner, the expectations at the time the courts of appeals were created seem to be confirmed, since the courts have taken an active decision making stance. Not only do they terminate most appellate business, but they actively involve themselves in the decision making process through actions that inherently embody conflict with other institutions. Affirmations may also involve conflict, but reversal by definition represents nonconsensual behavior.

Not only is reversal utilized more frequently in some circuits than in others, but it is also a reaction to some district judges and not to others. These reversal-support patterns in the district-circuit are similar to those of the Supreme Court in its relationship to judges in the circuits, in which there is evidence that some judges have a consistently higher percentage of cases affirmed than others. A study of Chief Judge Edgerton of the court of appeals for the District of Columbia shows that there was a 60 per cent chance of getting a grant of certiorari when Judge Edgerton dissented, but only a 13 per cent chance when he wrote the majority opinion. In seventeen out of twenty-two cases in which he dissented, the Supreme Court reversed.[21]

Justice Frankfurter, writing on the retirement of Judge Magruder of the First Circuit, stated:

> Naturally enough, an important factor in the exercise of the Court's discretionary judgment is the weight of the opinion below. When petitions for certiorari from decisions in which Judge Magruder wrote have come before the Court, such has been the quality of his opinions, the persuasiveness of his reasoning, and the confinement of decision to its proper scope, that on more than one occasion one has been led to say to his brethren, "Were we to bring the case here, could we improve on Magruder?" [22]

[21] Simon Rosenzweig, "The Opinions of Judge Edgerton — A Study in the Judicial Process," 37 Cornell Law Quarterly (1952), pp. 165–166.

[22] Felix Frankfurter, "Calvert Magruder," 72 Harvard Law Review (1959), p. 1202.

As a circuit judge reviewing district court actions, Judge Magruder agreed: "If the district court has written a careful full opinion with which we agree and which we feel unable to improve upon, we should affirm on the opinion of the court below." [23] Thus, a reviewing judge does consider the author of the original decision. We can therefore suggest that decision making in the appellate courts gives major consideration to individual district judges.

In the sample circuits, the rate of reversal over individual district judges' civil liberties decisions ranged from 0 to 100 per cent in the Third and Eighth and 0 to 80 per cent in the Fifth. Five judges in the Third Circuit — Follmer, Forman, McIlvane, Worthendyke, and Van Dusen — had all of their civil liberty decisions confirmed by the appellate court, whereas Judge Madden had all of his appealed cases overturned. In the Fifth Circuit, three judges — Sloan, Connally, and Davis — received complete approval by the appellate bench, whereas Judge Mize saw four of his five appealed decisions overturned. In the Eighth Circuit, Judges Ridge, Hicklin, Mickelson, Vogel, and Whittaker had all of their decisions confirmed, and Judge Young lost his three cases. If 22.7 per cent is taken as the average rate of reversal, ten judges out of nineteen exceeded this rate in the Third, nineteen out of thirty-two in the Fifth, and five out of sixteen in the Eighth. Therefore, both for individual districts and individual judges, the lowest level of support given by circuit to district occurred in the Fifth Circuit.

The reversal rate of circuit over district judges does not appear to have any relationship to the number of cases appealed. Judge Follmer in the Third Circuit had seventeen cases appealed, more than any other district judge in the circuit. Yet, all of his decisions were confirmed by the appellate court. Likewise, Judge Hooper in the Fifth Circuit had thirty-five decisions appealed, leading the circuit in the number of cases appealed, but had only four overturned (11.4 per cent). Thus, the number of cases appealed from a judge does not provide any clue to the support which will be given by the appellate court.

It is significant, however, that the variation in approval over dis-

[23] Calvert Magruder, "The Trials and Tribulations of an Intermediate Appellate Court," 44 *Cornell Law Quarterly* (1958), p. 3.

trict judges goes to such extremes. A judge who can see seventeen cases appealed and suffer no rebuffs must have greater status in the judicial power structure than a judge who sees all of his decisions overturned. The appellate task of bringing district decisions into line with national standards does not equally touch all parochial jurists in the district courts. Some receive remarkable support from their appellate colleagues; others, none at all.

It is not unusual for the conflicting ideologies of district and circuit judges to become a part of court record in reversal cases. After District Judge T. Whitfield Davidson, eighty-two-year old segregationist, repeatedly refused to implement the Dallas desegregation plan, claiming that it "would lead, in the opinion and the light of history and unquestionable sources to an amalgamation of the races," the Fifth Circuit reversed him for the sixth time, holding him directly responsible for the "frustrating history of this litigation." [24] Likewise, in the James Meredith case, Judge Wisdom of the Fifth Circuit, writing the reversal of District Judge Sidney Mize, condemned the trial judge for "unreasonably long delays" and "continuences of a doubtful propriety." Some intercourt conflict between circuits and districts arises because of differences in constituency and judicial roles. As Circuit Judge John R. Brown noted, "Lifetime tenure insulates judges from anxiety over worldly cares for body and home and family. But it does not protect them from the unconscious urge for the approbation of their fellow man, and fellow man most often means those of like interest and backgrounds, business and professional experiences and predilections, and even prejudices." [25] Since the favor of fellow man is different for many circuit and district judges, intercourt conflict develops.

Policy Direction of Review

The dominating motive for appeal of cases is generally an expectation — sometimes remote, sometimes probable — that previous deci-

[24] See Jack Peltason, *Fifty-Eight Lonely Men* (New York: Harcourt, Brace and World, 1961), pp. 122–126.

[25] John R. Brown, "Hail to the Chief: Hutcheson, the Judge," 38 *Texas Law Review* (1959), p. 145.

sions will be reversed and a change of policy effected. The number of reversals in the courts of appeals indicates that changes in political direction are frequent and that the political impact of such changes is great. The patterns of review established by the appeals courts may support other institutional decision makers and confirm their political judgments, or they may establish a different set of values.

The behavior of appellate decision makers in the sample of civil liberties cases indicates that they perform their role primarily by revising nonlibertarian cases from the district court. Table 6 shows the number of libertarian and nonlibertarian cases appealed in each circuit and the number and percentages overturned.

Libertarian and Nonlibertarian Cases Appealed and Reversed by Circuits [a]   TABLE 6

Circuit	Libertarian Cases Appealed	Overturned	Percentage of Reversal
Third	9	4	(44.4)
Fifth	36	11	(30.6)
Eighth	6	1	(16.7)

Circuit	Nonlibertarian Cases Appealed	Overturned	Percentage of Reversal
Third	111	29	(26.1)
Fifth	355	105	(30.0)
Eighth	132	28	(21.2)

[a] As used here, a libertarian decision is one made for the civil liberty claimed; a nonlibertarian decision is one made against the civil liberty claimed.
Source: Sample of cases.

Although the percentage of libertarian and nonlibertarian cases reversed in each circuit is comparable, only a relatively small number of district court decisions which uphold civil liberty claims are appealed to the United States courts of appeals. This suggests that once a liberty is granted in the district court the judicial process usually stops, and that the major purpose of the appellate courts is to review claims denied rather than granted. If the appellate courts do reverse, they are automatically more liberal, since nonlibertarian appeals are the lion's share of their docket. Since a purpose of creating the appellate courts was to review and broaden the decisions of the district courts to conform to national rather than parochial values, it appears that in the reversal of nonlibertarian district decisions, the appellate courts are performing this function.

In the case of labor, the behavior of the circuits is mixed. Although the Third Circuit demonstrates a greater response to the prolabor positions, by reversing more antilabor cases than prolabor cases, a radically different picture is presented in the Fifth, and to a lesser degree in the Eighth. In the Fifth Circuit a much higher percentage of prolabor district court and agency cases are reversed toward the antilabor position as shown in Table 7.

Prolabor and Antilabor Cases Appealed and Reversals by Circuits   TABLE 7

Circuit	Prolabor Cases Appealed	Overturned	Percentage of Reversal
Third	66	9	13.6
Fifth	143	60	42.0
Eighth	32	9	28.1

Circuit	Antilabor Cases Appealed	Overturned	Percentage of Reversal
Third	91	21	23.1
Fifth	150	39	26.0
Eighth	35	9	25.7

Source: Sample of cases.

Intracourt Behavior in Decision Making

Although district decisions are generally made by single judges, appeal decisions are the outcome of decision making processes involving groups of three judges. Since much of the litigation is controversial, we would expect appeals judges to behave differently both in their reaction to policy issues and their relationship with other institutions. Given differences in socio-political backgrounds, appeals judges should vary in their responses to controversial situations.

Therefore, investigation of reversals alone tells us little about the collegial conflict and consensus within the United States courts of appeals. Indeed, too great a reliance on district-circuit-Supreme Court relationships for explanation of reversals and affirmations may suggest that appellate benches react unitedly against inferior levels of the judicial hierarchy or administrative agencies. The relationships within the judicial system are much more complex, especially when viewed against the background of conflict in the collegial courts. The internal politics of the court tells us not only something about the institutional character of the judicial process, but also something of the structure of interpersonal relationships in the judicial system.

Table 8 describes the paucity of dissent in the three courts of appeals; only in the Fifth is the rate of dissent very significant. Even in the Fifth Circuit the comparatively high rate of dissent may be contrasted to the general average of Supreme Court dissents, which is often 50 per cent. Offhand, we would expect civil liberties and labor cases to be a prolific source of dissent, involving as

Appellate Dissents When Reversing and
Affirming Lower Court Decisions:
Civil Liberties and Labor Cases   TABLE 8

Circuit	Affirmed — Civil Liberties Per Cent Cases with Dissent	Reversed — Civil Liberties Per Cent Cases with Dissent
Third	2.3 (2 of 87)	15.2 (5 of 33)
Fifth	8.7 (24 of 275)	27.7 (31 of 116)
Eighth	3.7 (4 of 109)	0.0 (0 of 29)

Circuit	Affirmed — Labor Per Cent Cases with Dissent	Reversed — Labor Per Cent Cases with Dissent
Third	7.9 (10 of 127)	6.7 (2 of 30)
Fifth	9.8 (19 of 194)	14.1 (14 of 99)
Eighth	2.0 (1 of 49)	11.1 (2 of 18)

Source: Sample of cases.

they do many of the most controversial cases of recent political history. In the Fifth and Eighth Circuits, the civil liberties litigation was especially intense. However, our data corroborate other findings that dissent is simply not a frequent decision making pattern in the courts of appeals. An important line of inquiry is the relationship of dissent on the courts to their review of lower court and agency decisions; it enables us to examine the likelihood of conflict when the courts affirm or reverse various kinds of lower court decisions.

Table 8 suggests some important political characteristics of the federal courts, and describes some relationships between internal dissent and institutional review. We learn that dissent on the circuit courts is primarily a function of the reversal of lower court decisions; this is the case on both the Third and Fifth Circuits in the civil liberties sample but not on the Eighth, where there is simply very little dissent. When reversing civil liberties decisions from the district courts, the Fifth Circuit is three times more likely to be in conflict than when affirming cases; on the Third Circuit the court is more than six times as likely to be in conflict.

Internal conflict in the appellate courts that is strong enough to bring forth dissenting opinion is more often expressed by an appellate judge who agrees with a district judge while the majority of the circuit court wants to reverse. Since the reversal of civil liberties cases by the circuit courts is mainly directed toward turning nonlibertarian decisions into libertarian ones, we suggest that dissent in the lower appellate courts is usually an expression of nonlibertarianism. Table 9 permits an inspection of the libertarian-nonlibertarian nature of dissent.

The role of dissent in civil liberties cases in the appellate courts suggests that at least for two of the circuits, dissent, when exercised, occurs in a higher percentage of cases when the district court decision is being reversed rather than affirmed; and since appellate courts tend to hear and reverse more nonlibertarian cases, dissent in reversed cases is almost always an expression of nonlibertarianism.

Although dissent also occurs often in reversal of labor cases, its role is somewhat different than in the civil liberties sample, as shown in Table 10.

Civil Liberties: Distribution of Reversed Cases
Among Libertarian-Nonlibertarian and
Unanimous-Not Unanimous Positions   TABLE 9

	Percentage in Each Circuit		
Reversed Cases	Third (N = 33)	Fifth (N = 116)	Eighth (N = 29)
Reversing libertarian decisions in district court:			
Unanimous	12.1	10.3	3.4
Not unanimous	0.0	1.0	0.0
Reversing nonlibertarian decisions in district court:			
Unanimous	72.7	61.9	96.6
Not unanimous	15.2	26.8	0.0

Source: Sample of cases.

Labor: Distribution of Reversed Cases
Among Prolabor-Antilabor and
Unanimous-Not Unanimous Positions   TABLE 10

	Percentage in Each Circuit		
Reversed Cases	Third (N = 30)	Fifth (N = 99)	Eighth (N = 18)
Reversing prolabor decisions in lower court:			
Unanimous	23.3	51.5	38.0
Not unanimous	6.7	9.1	11.1
Reversing antilabor decisions in lower court:			
Unanimous	70.0	34.3	50.0
Not unanimous	0.0	5.0	0.0

Source: Sample of cases.

Dissent in labor cases in the three circuits is more often in a pro-labor direction. This is explained to some degree by the differential behavior exhibited by all the circuits in the labor cases, in contrast with their civil liberties docket. Certainly less prolabor support than procivil liberties support is given by the circuits. The most obvious example, of course, is in the Fifth Circuit, which, while maintaining a libertarian position on many civil liberties cases, is often anti-labor, reflecting to some degree the position of Chief Judge Joseph Hutcheson. Attacking the National Labor Relations Board, he called it, "a picture of administration at its most unjudicial worst, administration which, keeping the promise of a fair hearing to the ear, breaks it to the heart." [26] His opinion was shared by some of his colleagues, as revealed in the number of prolabor administrative agency decisions which were reversed by the Fifth Circuit on appeal. In the Third and Eighth Circuits, internal conflict occurred only in reversing prolabor district dicisions. In the Fifth, however, not only were more prolabor cases reversed unanimously, but when antilabor decisions were reversed, there was substantial dissent.

Collegial Decision Making

Records of dissent inform us about the nature of conflict in the judicial system. Dissent is also potentially useful for locating voting blocs within the collegial court and relating these blocs to other supporting blocs in the judiciary. Other factors besides the low rate of dissent, however, suggest the difficulties involved in sociometric analysis in the circuit courts.

Basic to the difficulty of dissent analysis in the circuit courts is their institutional structure of decision making. Whereas the Supreme Court regularly sits as a body in all cases and individual absences are exceptional in the decision making process, the circuit courts routinely hear cases in panels of three judges. Moreover, there is no obvious structure or consistency in the make-up of the three-judge committee and the group composition continually shifts and changes. Since there are only three judges to a panel, except in rare instances of *en banc* deliberations, the objective probability of dissent is much less than on a court of nine judges. Furthermore, a

---

[26] See "Joseph C. Hutcheson, Jr., Chief Judge, Fifth Circuit Court of Appeals," 35 *American Bar Association Journal* (1949), pp. 546 ff. See also Jack Peltason, *Federal Courts in the Political Process* (New York: Random House, 1955), pp. 16–17.

judge, when he dissents, always dissents alone. The intrinsic loneliness of dissent on the circuits may well act as a deterrent to a judge who faces the possibility of lone disagreement with the majority judges, in contrast to the Supreme Court, where a judge more frequently dissents in company with colleagues.

Of special importance in the analysis of conflict is the shifting context of dissent. On the Supreme Court, a dissenting judge usually reacts to a stable set of associates, and the interactions expressed by voting are in the context of the same justices; hence the context of dissent is relatively uniform. In the circuits, on the other hand, since the group context frequently changes, the judges with whom a dissenting judge disagrees continually change. Clearly, a dissent is in part a relational action, given the fact that one dissents from other judges. And when the relationships are unstable, as they are on the circuits, the significance of dissent is more ambiguous and difficult to measure. In the light of these facts, bloc analysis is not impossible, but it must be done with great care.

The paucity of dissent in the sample of civil liberties and labor cases precludes the use of bloc analysis. However, Goldman's studies of the courts of appeals have suggested the presence of organized voting patterns by the judges of the appellate courts along the lines of economic and political liberalism. He also found that party affiliation was associated with their voting behavior, especially on questions of economic liberalism.[27] That conflict and consensus in the courts of appeals are often along "conservative" and "liberal" lines conforms to the studies of voting behavior of the Supreme Court.

While intracourt conflict is most often seen in dissenting votes and bloc formation, the few *en banc* cases decided by the circuits offer some opportunity to study the court in conflict situations sitting together. Only eleven cases out of the total sample were

[27] Sheldon Goldman, "Voting Behavior of the United States Courts of Appeals, 1961–1964," 60 *American Political Science Review* (1966), pp. 374–383. See also Goldman, "Politics, Judges, and Administration of Justice: The Backgrounds, Recruitment, and Decisional Tendencies of the Judges of the United States Courts of Appeals, 1961–1964" (unpublished Ph.D. dissertation, Harvard University, 1965).

decided by the respective circuits sitting together, rather than in panels: three labor cases and two civil liberties in the Third Circuit; one labor and four civil liberties in the Fifth; and one civil liberties in the Eighth.[28]

In six of the seven civil liberties cases there were split decisions, and all four of the decisions in the labor cases were split. Thus, *en banc* deliberations represent a high degree of internal conflict on the court. The pattern of conflict in *en banc* deliberations closely follows the voting behavior of judges when operating in three-judge panels. For example, in the Fifth Circuit, Justice Ben Cameron was the most consistently antilibertarian member of the bench for years. His libertarian vote was the lowest in our sample of cases, and in the *en banc* cases he took the antilibertarian position in three out of four cases. Late in his career, Judge Cameron referred to four of his libertarian colleagues as "The Four," charging that panels were "rigged" to include them in civil rights litigation in order to obtain libertarian decisions.[29] In the *en banc* decisions in which he participated with them, three of "The Four"—Rives, Wisdom, and Tuttle—voted in a libertarian position. Two justices with mixed records in civil liberties litigation—Justices Hutcheson and Jones—voted twice in the antilibertarian position, twice in the libertarian position, in *en banc* cases. In the one labor case, Hutcheson and Cameron took an antilabor stance.[30]

These patterns of behavior were followed in *en banc* deliberations in other circuits. For example, in the Third Circuit, Justice Biggs took an antilabor position in all three *en banc* cases, and Justice Kalodner took a prolabor position in all three. In six of the seven

[28] Third Circuit: *King* v. *Waterman Ship Corporation* 272 F. 2d. 823; *Curtis* v. *Garcia* 272 F. 2d. 235; *N.L.R.B.* v. *U.S. Steel Corporation* 278 F. 2d. 896; *U.S. ex. rel. Silvio DeVita* v. *McCorkle* 248 F. 2d. 1; *Snyder* v. *Leheigh Valley Railroad* 245 F. 2d. 112; Fifth Circuit: *Noah* v. *Lib. Mutual Insurance Co.* 267 F. 2d. 218; *Shelton* v. *U.S.* 246 F. 2d. 571; *Howard* v. *U.S.* 232 F. 2d. 274; *Board of Supervisors* v. *Tureaud* 228 F. 2d. 895; *McKenna* v. *Ellis* 289 F. 2d. 928; Eighth Circuit: *Aaron* v. *Cooper* 257 F. 2d. 33.

[29] *Armstrong* v. *Board of Education of City of Birmingham*, Fifth Circuit, July 30, 1963, p. 15. See "Judicial Performance in the Fifth Circuit," 73 *Yale Law Journal* (1963), pp. 116–117.

[30] For an excellent summary of Fifth Circuit voting of judges see "Judicial Performance," pp. 120–122.

civil liberties cases, the court majority voted for a libertarian position, five times reversing the district courts. In the four labor cases,
the courts held twice for labor, twice against. Such results conform
very closely to the normal pattern of court behavior in three-judge
panels. In sum, *en banc* deliberations permit the normal differences
on the court to converge upon one case and be sharply revealed.

The foregoing pages, by an exploration of the institutional character and decision making behavior of the United States courts of
appeals, have suggested some of the major characteristics of appellate litigation in the federal judicial system. We have seen that
the appellate docket is heavy, that screening of the docket takes
place, and that the number of cases decided per judge is not great.
We have found that although a filtering takes place in the appeals
courts, more important is that the appellate process sometimes trans-
forms and increases political issues in litigation. We have also seen
that, whereas most cases may be legally appealed, in fact, nonlibertarian cases are appealed and reversed, and, except for the
Fifth Circuit, antilabor cases primarily are appealed and reversed.
In addition, although legal opportunity is provided for dissent in
all cases, dissent is primarily a support for district courts when
reversing nonlibertarian decisions. The panel structure of the appeals
courts has major effect upon judges' behavior, and the conflicts
appearing in panel deliberations are revealed and reinforced most
clearly in *en banc* cases.

THE LOWER COURTS AND
THE SUPREME COURT

As our best known judicial institution, the Supreme Court has been carefully studied. Its decisions and judicial behavior have usually, however, been examined in isolation from the judicial system of which it is a part. As a result a somewhat fragmented view of the judicial system has emerged. Although linked together by a process that involves frequent and regular relationships, the courts have seldom been investigated as a system of interactions. Since, as Schubert has observed, "probably the least amount of work has been done in regard to the relationships between sets of judges," [1] the Supreme Court's linkages with lower federal courts have not been systematically described and are theoretically ambiguous.

[1] Glendon Schubert, *Judicial Behavior: A Reader in Theory and Research* (Chicago: Rand McNally, 1964), p. 190.

CHAPTER SEVEN

To the degree that intercourt relationships are discussed in judicial studies, the view of the judicial system seems largely formal and legal, synthesized from the codes and statutes. Implicit in most writing on the federal judiciary is the hierarchical theory.[2] This model looks at the judicial system as a hierarchy of courts with the Supreme Court at the apex in command of the judicial system.

[2] This section is taken from Kenneth N. Vines, "The Role of Circuit Courts of Appeal in the Federal Judicial Process: A Case Study," 7 *Midwest Journal of Political Science* (1963), pp. 306–307. Among those works which seem to rely on the hierarchical theory are Alpheus Mason and William Beaney, *American Constitutional Law* (New York: Prentice-Hall, 1964); Wallace Mendelson, *The Constitution and the Supreme Court* (New York: Dodd, Mead, 1966); Carl Swisher, *American Constitutional Development* (Boston: Houghton, Mifflin, 1943).

According to this view the judicial process proceeds from the district courts, through intermediary courts, and finally to the Supreme Court where, at last, authoritative decisions are made. Belief in the hierarchical theory doubtless explains the extreme "upper court bias" in American political science, the emphasis upon Supreme Court activities to the comparative neglect of the activities of other courts. Another consequence of the belief in the hierarchical theory is the conception of constitutional law as that body of decisions which the Supreme Court hands down, a notion not supported by any really systematic researches. Of course, if the hierarchical theory were correct, such distortions would be largely justified, since all important decisions would be made in the Supreme Court at the top of the hierarchy, while the lower courts, participating in the chain of command, would play an interesting but by no means important role in the judicial process.

A second theory, closely related to the hierarchical idea, holds that policy making in the federal courts is best conceived of as the Supreme Court interacting with a bureaucracy of lower courts.[3] This analogy, drawn from the political theory of the executive, suggests that the Supreme Court makes the important decisions, which are then put into effect more or less efficiently by its judicial bureaucracy. While this view allocates more power to the lower courts than the hierarchical theory, the power consists of that residue of inefficiency and recalcitrance in the activities of a bureaucracy.

Both theories describe important phases of the federal judicial process. Studies of constitutional politics have shown that the judicial process does form hierarchical patterns with instances where the Supreme Court acts as final arbiter. At times the Supreme Court and the lower courts do interact as if the lower courts were the highest court's bureaucracy. But most of the work of the lower courts seems less dependent on the Supreme Court than either the hierarchical or bureaucracy theories would indicate. Cases remanded to the lower courts often allow wide latitude in the imple-

[3] An articulate statement of the bureaucratic theory may be found in Walter Murphy, "Chief Justice Taft and the Lower Court Bureaucracy: A Study in Judicial Administration," 24 *Journal of Politics* (1962), pp. 453–477.

mentation of Supreme Court decisions and the norms and policies inculcated in lower court decisions may be virtually unrecognizable as descendants of the original Supreme Court decision.[4] Moreover, it is not clear that the Supreme Court is handling the same policies that are involved in the thousands of cases heard in the lower courts each year. Of all the lower court cases, the Supreme Court can hear only between one and two hundred a year, including the few appealable to it by right and the relatively small number it perceives to be of wide public or governmental interest. Thus, by its very nature the certiorari process of selection is much less a scientific sampling procedure of business in the lower courts than an informed series of personal judgments. In consequence the lower courts may be handling quite different policy questions, responding to different pressures, and resolving different conflicts than the Supreme Court.

The studies of lower court activity in desegregation litigation certainly confirm that much less supervision is imposed upon the lower courts by the Supreme Court than either the hierarchical or bureaucratic theories would indicate.[5] Avoidance, delay, and outright defiance of Supreme Court rulings were all too often a pattern among lower courts in this critical policy area. This suggests that other assumptions of "judicial hierarchy" deserve exploration, including (1) access to the Supreme Court through the system and its appellate or review role; (2) the decisional involvement with the lower courts by the Supreme Court; (3) the resolution of conflict within the system by the Supreme Court; (4) the direction of Supreme Court review and its role in the system; and (5) the movement of personnel within the system.

To investigate these features of the judicial system, we will utilize two samples of cases. First, we will investigate the sample of civil liberties and labor issues explored in the district and appellate courts earlier in relation to their appeal to the Supreme Court. And

---

[4] A classic example is the school desegregation case, *Brown* v. *Board of Education of Topeka,* 347 U.S. 483 (1954).

[5] See Jack Peltason, *Fifty-Eight Lonely Men* (New York: Harcourt, Brace and World, 1961), and Albert Blaustein and Clarence Ferguson, *Desegregation and the Law* (New Brunswick: Rutgers University Press, 1957).

second, we will look at lower federal court antecedents for the entire Supreme Court's docket for 1964 and 1965.

Access to the Supreme Court

Frankfurter and Landis, writing on access to the Supreme Court, emphasized its interdependence with the remainder of the judiciary with the reminder that "the work of the Supreme Court is largely predetermined by the jurisdictional ambit of the lower courts." [6] While the Constitution provides for certain cases to be heard in original jurisdiction, Congress determines the categories of cases which shall be heard and from what institutions these shall come. In consequence, while the instances of original jurisdiction have remained unchanged, congressional statutes have decisively shaped the remaining methods by which the docket of the court is formed and access is permitted.

At the present time there are three distinct methods by which access to the Court is obtained, two of them linked to the lower federal courts. These are: (1) Cases heard by right of original jurisdiction as provided in Article III of the Constitution. Cases explicitly named for consideration are narrowly limited to controversies involving ambassadors, other public ministers and consuls, and those in which states are opposing litigants. (2) Cases heard by right of appeal from lower federal courts or state courts. Two important categories are cases involving the constitutionality of federal statutes and of state statutes. (3) Cases that are selected by the Court through writs of certiorari from among those appealed to it from state courts (cases involving federal questions), and from other federal courts.

In two instances the Court gets cases after they have been filed, tried, and decided in lower courts; in the third, cases heard in original jurisdiction come to the Court *de novo* and are decided there. The narrow definition of cases to be heard in original jurisdiction or through appeals as of right suggests that these two

[6] Felix Frankfurter and James Landis, *The Business of the Supreme Court* (New York: Macmillan, 1927), pp. 2–3.

categories contribute a minority of the Court's business. This supposition is borne out by a survey of cases for the 1959–60 term.

While state courts contribute a sizeable share of the Supreme Court's litigation, many of the decisions are not regarded as meriting an extended explanation. Hence, they are frequently decided through per curiam opinions usually involving no more than half a page. On the other hand, the largest group of signed opinions of length and substance are most frequently cases from the federal courts that are heard by writ of certiorari. Of the ninety-five signed opinions, 80 per cent came from federal courts; all but three of these federal cases in signed opinions were from lower rather than special courts.

Access to the Supreme Court involves, as shown in Table 1, substantial linkages with both state and lower federal courts. In cases meriting extended opinion and attention by the Court, lower federal cases are predominant. And in both state and federal access routes, certiorari provides a primary tool by which the Supreme Court may restrict or open access.

Origin of Cases in Supreme Court, 1959–60
Term by Character of Opinion   TABLE 1

	Original Jurisdiction	Appeal as of Right		Certiorari	
		State	*Federal*	*State*	*Federal*
Per curiam	0	63	21	16	35
Signed	2	9	13	8	63
	(2) .8%	(72) 31.3%	(34) 14.8%	(24) 10.4%	(98) 42.7%

Source: *United States Reports,* 1959–60.

Certiorari was designed primarily to increase the Court's control over its policy function by reducing its involvement in appeals litigation. Instead of automatic access to the Court, restriction was placed requiring a certification of cases by an affirmative vote of four of the judges on the court. Professor Joseph Tanenhaus has shown the political cues involved in the certification vote.[7] The Court's Rule 19 sets up some formal guidelines for certification, such as conflict in the circuits, departure of lower court rulings from a Supreme Court ruling or from local decisions, or the existence of an important question not yet decided by the Court. However, important political cues not mentioned in Rule 19, such as identity of the plaintiff, the subject matter of the case, and the political structure of the lower courts' decisions, also frequently are correlated with the decision to grant certiorari.

The usual rationale in the operation of certiorari is that the Court chooses from among the numerous applications for appeal those cases of important national interest, thus performing an important screening function. The number selected is only a comparatively small portion of those appealed, for example, about 200 of the 1862 cases that were appealed in the 1959 term. The discretionary nature of the certiorari process is indicated by the character of the cases selected for review. The Court's selection often omits important policy cases, for legal experts have demonstrated that quite different choices could logically have been made. Harper and Rosenthal have indicated that in the 1949 term the Court did not hear sixty-four cases involving important policy issues, most of them from the lower federal courts. These sixty-four cases represented many categories of litigation and included twenty-two civil rights cases, five citizenship and alien status cases, four labor cases, four tax cases, seven antitrust cases, three trade and patent cases, and one admiralty case. Similar conclusions were reached in a study of certiorari for the 1950 term.[8] One case not reviewed in the 1950 term was the Alger Hiss case and Richard Nixon was quoted as saying that the Supreme Court's refusal to hear the case certified Hiss's guilt.

Since the Court hears only about 15 per cent of the cases appealed

[7] Joseph Tanenhaus, Marvin Schick, Matthew Muraskin, and Daniel Rosen, "The Supreme Court's Certiorari Jurisdiction: Cue Theory," in Glendon Schubert, ed., *Judicial Decision-Making* (New York: Free Press of Glencoe, 1963), pp. 115 ff.

[8] Fowler V. Harper and Alan S. Rosenthal, "What the Supreme Court Did Not Do During the 1950 Term," 100 *University of Pennsylvania Law Review* (1951), pp. 354–409.

to it from the lower courts, and since appellate applications increase yearly, the percentage of cases will probably decline still further. This suggests that the Supreme Court is systematically reducing its appellate review and supervisory role over the court system. At present there are no plans, such as the addition of judges or changes in structure, that would make it feasible to hear more cases. Intervention by the Supreme Court in the day-to-day functioning of the judicial process is less likely as litigation increases and review decreases.

The Supreme Court's Limited Appellate Role

In contrast to the appellate load of the Supreme Court, 3,713 appeals were tried in the courts of appeals during 1960, 82.9 per cent of them from the district courts and the remainder from special courts and administrative agencies. Comparing the appellate functions of Supreme Court and courts of appeals for 1960, the higher court handled 6.2 per cent as many cases as did the lower appeals courts. As legal authorities have testified, important political and legal questions are decided in the courts of appeals when the Supreme Court refuses certiorari. Doubtless, also, important policy questions are decided in the courts of appeals that are not appealed further for lack of motivation, time, or resources.

These considerations emphasize that the Supreme Court is not primarily a court of review, although it does fulfill some appellate functions. The appellate cases heard by the Court do not embody any systematic fulfillment of appellate needs or any objective selection of important appeals cases. At the present time, there is little intention that the Court should fulfill an appellate function. The act of 1925 culminated a calculated effort by Congress to transform the Court from a work-a-day appellate tribunal to a more selective policy role.

The popular statement that one will appeal a case "all the way to the Supreme Court" is somewhat of a popular myth to the extent that it symbolizes the court's appellate function. A more realistic and accurate statement would be the assertion that the case will be appealed "all the way to the court of appeals." For it is in these courts that the appellate function is systematically fulfilled. The dominant appellate role of the intermediate court is sanctioned by legal theory. Chief Justice Taft has noted that the appellate process is essentially a two-step affair and that "the sound theory . . . is that litigants have their rights sufficiently protected by a hearing or trial in the courts of the first instance, and by one review in an intermediate appellate court."[9] This statement was made at the time of the passage of the act of 1925 which drastically limited the appellate function of the Supreme Court. Moreover, the act insured that the appellate function would be adequately fulfilled even though the court would not be performing it.

To the degree therefore, that the theory of judicial hierarchy ascribes to the Supreme Court a review of all lower court activity, or all lower court errors, or all important judicial cases, it is inaccurate. The appellate court role is not a primary function of the Supreme Court.

Conflict Resolution in the Judicial System

Varying patterns of conflict and agreement result from the cases that are appealed from the district courts to the regional courts of appeals. In a small group of these that it elects to hear, the Supreme Court carries the judicial process a step further by intervening in the decisional relationships among the lower courts.

Only about one out of five cases heard by the Court involves any sort of conflict among the circuits or conflict with the Supreme Court in line with the criteria of Rule 19. Other important kinds of conflict in the lower courts occur, however, namely differences between district and appeals courts and conflicts between lower court judges. The reaction of the Supreme Court to these conflicts is of interesting political significance.

Within the context of the hierarchical model of the judicial system, one may assume that the Supreme Court plays the role of arbitrator of conflict. That is, one of its primary roles is to resolve conflict between and among the lower courts in order to have a uniform

[9] William H. Taft, "The Jurisdiction of the Supreme Court Under the Act of February 13, 1925," 35 *Yale Law Review* (1926), p. 2.

standard of law throughout the federal system. Certainly, the interests of the legal subculture promote such a role for the court. From these assumptions, a number of interesting testable hypotheses arise:

1. In the Supreme Court's limited docket, more cases involve conflict (differences) between district courts and courts of appeals, than cases of consensus (agreement) between the two levels of lower courts.

2. The Supreme Court is more inclined to both hear and reverse a decision in which there is lower court difference than those in which lower courts are in agreement.

3. Of the cases heard, more cases will be included in which the appellate court was divided (indicating conflict among the three-judge panel) than cases in which it was unanimous.

4. The Supreme Court will be more frequently inclined to reverse cases in which the appeals court was divided than those in which the appeals court was unanimous.

5. Finally, when the Supreme Court hears a case in which the appeals court and the district court are in disagreement, it will more often support the appeals court than the district court.

To test these assumptions and to investigate the role of the Supreme Court as arbitrator of intrasystem conflict, we will look at the lower court antecedents of all cases on the Supreme Court's docket for 1964 and 1965 that came up through the basic lower court system from the district court to the courts of appeals to the Supreme Court. All other cases, including state, bureaucratic appeals, and original jurisdiction, have been excluded. The results of this investigation are included in Table 2.[10] Of the 157 cases in the two-year time period that had complete lower court antecedents, it was possible to locate lower court information on all but 7, for a total sample of 150.

In cases brought through the system the Court is always respond-

[10] The authors are indebted to Carl Lee Swidorski, undergraduate at Western Michigan University, for collection of data in this section and for use of material from his honors thesis.

Cases Reaching the Supreme Court Through
Federal Appellate Route 1964–1965   TABLE 2

| | Supreme Court Votes for Affirmation | | Supreme Court Votes for Reversal | |
Circuit	Affirmed Consensus	Arbitrated Conflict in Favor of the Circuit Court	Reversed Consensus	Arbitrated Conflict in Favor of the District Court
First	0	0	2	1
Second	7	5	9	7
Third	3	2	1	4
Fourth	3	2	3	2
Fifth	7	2	10	9
Sixth	5	0	9	2
Seventh	1	2	9	3
Eighth	2	1	4	1
Ninth	1	2	9	0
Tenth	1	0	4	2
District of Columbia	2	0	10	1
Totals	32	16	70	32

Source: *United States Reports*, 1964 and 1965.

ing to an opinion delivered in the courts below. The *raison d'être* for the appeal is that the decision below will be reviewed and resolved with an opinion that either agrees or disagrees with the courts below. The process of review requires study of both the trial records and previous opinions. In both instances it is inevitable that the Supreme Court's perceptions of the case will be influenced by its previous history and that the Court will respond to its previous record. A variety of responses are possible, ranging from a disapproving or reluctant reversal to a grudging or admiring affirmation. Thus, the Supreme Court makes its decisions in the context of lower court determinations, conflicts, and case structures.

In reacting to appellate decisions the Court achieves several different kinds of political results. If district and appeals court agree it may either confirm this agreement or introduce conflict into the system by reversing. On the other hand, if district and appeals court disagree it can decide this conflict by endorsing the decision of either court. The role of the Court in arbitrating conflict seems especially significant. If disagreement occurs among local district courts and regional appeals courts, such conflict is an aspect of controversy in the federal system. According to traditional expectation an important task of the Supreme Court is the arbitration of conflict in the federal system when it occurs in the judicial process as well as elsewhere. If, however, the district and appeals courts agree, the Supreme Court can disrupt this consensus by reversing both courts, a significant action in an interdependent system.

The data contained in Table 2 present interesting information on the problem posed earlier, namely the role of the Supreme Court in arbitrating conflict between the district and appeals courts. The data indicate that the Supreme Court primarily heard cases in which the district and circuit courts agreed, 102 of 150 cases (68 per cent). Thus its docket is so constructed that only about a third of the cases involved conflict between district and appeals courts while about two-thirds showed the courts in agreement. Of these 102 cases of consensus, the Court reversed the lower court agreement 70 times (70 per cent). Thus, of the 150 total case sample, the Supreme Court introduced conflict into the system 47 per cent of the time. We can say that the Supreme Court hears more cases in which lower courts agree and reverses a high percentage of this agreement. Table 3 shows a similar tendency for our six-year sample of civil liberties and labor cases reviewed by the Supreme Court.

From these data, we can conclude that the most numerous category of cases by which the Court interacted with lower courts in-

Supreme Court Responses to Civil Liberties and
Labor Cases from Three Circuits (N = 39)   TABLE 3

	Percentage
Affirmed consensus of lower courts	26
Reversed consensus of lower courts	46
Affirmed appeals court in conflict	10
Reversed appeals court in conflict	18

Source: Sample of cases.

volved the substitution of its own judgment for the agreement
reached by lower courts. The federal appellate process thus em-
bodies a policy interplay among different levels of the courts, in
which the Supreme Court often plays a role as disrupter of policy
consensus coming from the lower courts.

When the Supreme Court was cast in a role of arbitrator of conflict, an interesting feature of its behavior in both samples of cases
was its more frequent reversal of appeals courts decisions in favor
of the district court position. Table 2 shows twice as many cases
reversed in favor of the district court as appeals court. One would
assume, perhaps, in conflicts between level of courts that the Supreme Court would be more supportive of the less localized agents.
A "bureaucratic" view of the system would, it seems, indicate that
more "superior" bureaucrats would be more often supported in
disputes than "inferiors." Evidently, in instances of conflict where
appeals courts decisions were "satisfactory," they were not selected
for review as frequently. On the other hand, in cases in which the
district courts interpreted the issues more in accordance with the
Supreme Court perceptions than the appeals court did, for example
in labor cases, the Court was more inclined to review lower court
conflict situations. In those cases the Court often confirmed the
action of the district court, but sometimes on grounds different than
those the district court used.

Two additional questions were raised on conflict resolution: Is
the docket of the Supreme Court composed of more cases in which
the appeals court was divided than unanimous and second, is it
more inclined to reverse a case from a split appeals court as opposed
to a unanimous decision. Table 4 offers information on these
questions. The Supreme Court heard a total of thirty-five cases in
the federal route in which the appellate court was divided representing 23 per cent of the total of 150 cases appealed through the
regular route. Therefore, a large majority (77 per cent) of the cases
were appealed from unanimous appellate courts.

The Supreme Court reversed twenty-four of the split decisions
(69 per cent). In cases appealed from unanimous appellate courts it
reversed 78 of 115 cases (68 per cent). Thus, there is almost no
difference in the reversal rates for split decisions and unanimous

*Split Decisions in Circuit Cases Appealed to
Supreme Court 1964–1965, by Circuit*   TABLE 4

Circuit	Split Decisions	Affirmed	Reversed
First	1	0	1
Second	9	2	7
Third	2	1	1
Fourth	6	2	4
Fifth	7	3	4
Sixth	1	0	1
Seventh	2	1	1
Eighth	0	0	0
Ninth	3	1	2
Tenth	1	1	0
District of Columbia	3	0	3
Totals	35	11	24

Source: Same as Table 2.

decisions. Any hypothesis, therefore, that the Supreme Court hears more cases in which the appellate court is divided in its decision is not supported by this data. There is no evidence for a belief that the Court would be more likely to reverse a divided as opposed to a united appellate court. The Supreme Court hears many more unanimous appeals than split ones and reverses almost equally the divided and united appellate courts.

The reaction of the Supreme Court to split decisions in the appellate court suggests that it is not primarily guided by lower court agreement — either intercourt or intracourt — in deciding the cases it will hear or reverse. The Supreme Court affirmed consensus in thirty-two cases appealed through the federal route, seven of which were split decisions (22 per cent). It reversed consensus seventy times, thirteen of which were split decisions (19 per cent). Likewise, of the thirty-two cases in which it arbitrated conflict in favor of the district courts, eleven were split decisions (34 per cent), and of the sixteen cases in which it arbitrated conflict in favor of the circuit courts, four were split decisions (25 per cent). These data show that the smallest percentage of split decision cases were located in the group in which the Supreme Court was reversing consensus. Eighty-one per cent of the time that the Supreme Court was reversing the consensus of the two lower courts, it was reversing a united appellate court. Thus, with the major portion of its docket, the Supreme Court was acting entirely alone in articulating its decisional values, without any recorded support from any of the judges who sat on the circuit courts or on the district courts.

While the Supreme Court does perform a limited conflict resolution role in disputes between circuits, its handling of its docket often has an opposite effect on district-appellate conflict. To the degree that it reviews decisions at all, the Supreme Court's policy pronouncements are often in direct conflict with lower court rulings.

Utilization of Lower Court Opinions

We have noted that the Supreme Court gets a large majority of the important cases it hears from the lower federal courts and thus depends on these courts for prior legal definition and processing. In order to examine the impact of lower court opinions on those of the Supreme Court, we have gone to our sample of labor and civil liberties cases, selected those in the courts of appeals reviewed by the Supreme Court, and observed the extent of lower court involvement in the Court's opinions. There are several ways in which Supreme Court and lower courts may be linked. First, the Court may ignore lower court deliberations altogether, citing no data from the trial record and not discussing the merits of the opinions delivered in the courts below. A second possibility is that the Court may depend partially on lower court actions, citing the trial record, and referring briefly to the decisions. Third, the Court may rely heavily on lower court deliberations, citing lower court opinions at length, commenting on their merits, and depending on their opinions in deciding the case.

The thirty-nine cases that were heard in the Supreme Court from our sample evidenced the following degree of involvement with lower court opinions:

No mention of lower court   48.7 per cent (19 decisions)
Moderate reliance on lower court   15.4 per cent (6 decisions)
Extensive reliance on lower court   35.9 per cent (14 decisions)

In about half the opinions, no mention was made of lower court activity other than a passing formal reference in the opening declaration of the case. Of the remaining opinions, however, fourteen, or more than one-third, relied heavily on the opinions from the lower courts. Sometimes in these cases, the Court opinion was something of a dialogue in which the appeals courts (occasionally the district court) opinion was debated and cited in detail. In this category of cases it appears that Supreme Court decisions are molded by deliberations and decisions made in the courts below.

In six of the fourteen cases of extensive reliance, the function of the lower court citation was only to justify a dissenting opinion. In all such cases, the appeals court's opinions were cited as the correct view of the case and objection was made to overruling that opinion, a plea in one sense against judicial activism in the form of interfering with lower court decisions. In the remaining eight cases the majority opinion relied on lower court decisions; this was one-fifth (20.5 per cent) of the total number of cases.

Six of the eight cases in which the majority opinion dealt with the lower court deliberations involved conflict among the circuits; that is, they represented an issue on which appeals courts in different circuits had decided differently. Our findings here parallel those elsewhere that intercircuit conflict is present in only a small group of those cases chosen for review by the Supreme Court.

As other studies have shown, numerous instances of intercircuit conflict are not heard by the Court. Given the large amount of appellate business conducted in the circuits, the Supreme Court only samples intercircuit conflict, partly because the job of resolution is too much for a single court, and partly because the Court has wished to settle other kinds of policy issues more frequently. It is clear that the Court does not systematically supervise the judicial system but selectively inspects those problems and processes which fit in with the Court's policy making designs.

It is possible that more attention is paid to lower court decisions in conferences and discussions on the Court and that they are more influential in shaping Supreme Court decisions than appears in the actual opinions. Undoubtedly lower court opinions are read routinely as part of the process by which appeals are considered. For that matter, a good deal happens in the court process such as arguments, briefs, and suggested concepts that never appears in the opinion. What emerges in the opinion represents those concepts and that part of the process that the Court considers desirable to include in the record of the decision. Inclusion in the opinion, therefore, may be an index of the importance of lower court activities in the decision making process. An alternative hypothesis is that what is included in the opinions has been selected for its utility in rationalizing the selected policy result.

Direction of Review

Review of lower court decisions inevitably requires acting on their opinions. An affirmation of the decision below is a vote of confidence for the lower court whereas a reversal is a rebuke that nullifies the decisions and, at least in part, the work and justification that has gone into the opinion. Of great importance is the relation of Supreme Court review to the political tendencies of the appellate courts and more indirectly to the district courts as well. By review, policy patterns in the courts below can be modified or left undisturbed. Supreme Court consideration of our sample of labor and civil liberties is described in Table 5.

Relation of Court Review to
Appeals Courts Decisions   TABLE 5

	Percentage Reversed	Percentage Approved
Labor	80.0 (N = 12)	20.0 (N = 3)
Civil liberties	66.7 (N = 16)	33.3 (N = 8)

Source: Sample of cases.

In both policy areas, but particularly in labor cases, Court review disturbed decisional tendencies in the circuits by reversing a large majority of cases heard. Moreover, the direction of the reversals was predominantly in a direction favoring labor and granting the civil liberty claimed.

Of those cases reversed, 91.7 per cent of labor cases were for the labor claim (11 of 12 cases) and 100.0 per cent of civil liberties cases were for the civil liberty claimed (16 cases). Reversed cases tended, however, to come from some circuits more than others. Of the twelve labor cases reversed, eleven or 91.7 per cent came from the Fifth Circuit, and of the sixteen civil liberties cases reversed, ten or 62.5 per cent came from the Fifth Circuit.

These data indicate clearly that the Supreme Court used review of lower court decisions to liberalize the political stance of the Fifth Circuit both in civil liberties and in labor. That this relationship echoes national political tendencies is easy to see. In both congressional and state politics, Southern politicians tend to be unsympathetic to the interests of labor, often enacting such policies as "right to work" acts on the state level and voting against beneficent acts in the national Congress. Not surprisingly, Southern judges, recruited from Southern constituencies and having regional experiences, embody similar tendencies in their decisions.

Our sample represents, of course, only a small group of decisions from the total of 150 to 200 per year. Since labor and civil liberties represent problems of unusual national importance, however, the data suggest that a principal function of the Supreme Court is to nationalize the parochial values embodied in the decisions of the appeals courts.

Movement of Intrasystem Personnel

Within the federal judicial system, the movement or promotion of judges from one court level to another has been a constant concern of legal interests in American society. Using the rationale of "expertise," experience, and testing of judicial temperament, the American Bar Association has encouraged legislation requiring prior judicial experience for all federal judicial appointments. It is assumed, Professor Grossman has noted in his study of legal activities, that "prior judicial experience does give the recruiter a unique view of the ways in which a judge is likely to handle the new role."[11]

[11] Joel Grossman, *Lawyers and Judges* (New York: John Wiley, 1965), p. 202.

Judicial experience is also a major consideration of democratic interests for, as Professor Schubert has suggested, "promoting lower federal court judges to the Supreme Court betokens not so much a desire to create a career federal judiciary as it does an attempt to identify safe partisans whose ideological positions have been tried and proven in the minor leagues." [12]

A hierarchical conception of the judicial system would anticipate a substantial promotion of personnel upward to the Supreme Court, a system in which appellate courts are composed of talented and experienced former district judges and the Supreme Court composed of the most skilled former lower court jurists. Since the Supreme Court has no formal involvement in either the selection, removal, or promotion of lower judges, its hierarchical role in terms of personnel becomes somewhat suspect. When one considers the limited amount of lower court experience among Supreme Court justices and the paucity of judicial promotion, the organizational model of hierarchy becomes inoperative.

Professor Abraham's research indicates that among the ninety-six individual justices who served on the Supreme Court between 1789 and 1967, only twenty had ten or more years of previous judicial experience on any lower level, state or federal, at the time of their appointment and forty had no judicial experience at all.[13] Only twenty-two appointees had any lower federal court experience ranging from one to sixteen years.

The linkages therefore between the Supreme Court and lower federal courts in terms of personnel promotion are limited. Historically, this has resulted from views similar to those held by Justice Frankfurter that "the correlation between prior judicial experience and fitness for the Supreme Court is zero." [14] Thus, the district court judge is not necessarily the potentially competent appellate judge and lower court jurists are not necessarily the logical precursors of the Supreme Court justice. The Supreme Court is not

[12] Glendon Schubert, *Judicial Policy-Making* (Glenview: Scott, Foresman, 1965), p. 12.

[13] Henry J. Abraham, *The Judicial Process* (New York: Oxford University Press, 1968), p. 52.

[14] Felix Frankfurter, "The Supreme Court in the Mirror of Justices," 105 *University of Pennsylvania Law Review* (1957), p. 781.

just a higher order of the district and circuit courts and the selection of its personnel indicates its uniqueness. As Frankfurter noted, "not only is the framework within which the judicial process of the Supreme Court operates drastically different from the jurisdictional and procedural concerns of other courts, but the cases that now come before the court . . . present issues that make irrelevant considerations in the choice of Justices that at former periods had pertinence." [15]

To conclude, we have argued that the Supreme Court, in its relationship with the lower courts, does not, and probably cannot, fulfill the functions of a superior court of appeals in any adequate fashion. We have shown that the selection of the Supreme Court business is basically attuned to political factors and that access to the Court is restricted. We have also suggested that the court cannot supervise the lower courts in a thorough fashion, either in the performance of their day-to-day decision making or in their implementation of Supreme Court decisions. We have shown that the conflict resolution role ascribed to the Supreme Court in an intra-system context does not conform to the make-up of its docket nor the disposition of it. Finally, we have concluded that the lack of lower federal court experience for 80 per cent of the Supreme Court justices makes "judicial promotion" of less significance than we might have assumed.

In many respects, the court is best understood as a high court, similar to the Court of Appeals in England. It functions as a kind of national council of review which interacts with the lower courts, not as a systematic court of appeals or an adequate supervisor of the lower court system, but as a policy formulator for selected issues. Its task is public policy formation, using lower court decisions as its medium. It selectively inspects and responds to political tendencies in the lower courts, encouraging, modifying, and restricting the political patterns set in motion by litigation. Thus, the lower courts and Supreme Court do "articulate as a system," but the system is less structured and rigid than either the hierarchical or bureaucratic models suggest.

[15] *Ibid.*

CONCLUSIONS

The politics of federal courts, we have shown, involve a manifold of complex and significant lower court institutions. We have argued that their study requires theory attuned to their complexity and empirical research appropriate to their significance. To these ends our study has offered a theoretical model by which the courts can be more effectively investigated. Through the use of this model we have explored key features of their behavioral patterns and institutional practices. This research enables us to comment more meaningfully on the questions raised in Chapter One concerning both the utility of certain theories of the federal judiciary and problems involved in obtaining adequate empirical data for lower court analysis.

CHAPTER EIGHT

The Lower Court Subsystem

In Chapter One, we summed up the political and legal facets of the lower courts, their policy functions, and the influences that shape them in an integrated picture of the judicial subsystem. This model has helped to reveal activities in the lower judiciary that might otherwise be neglected. Its special value, however, has been to guide research toward the discovery of three major features of the lower court subsystem: (1) the complex and varied patterns of lower court behavior; (2) the involvement of legal and democratic subcultures; and (3) the interrelatedness of all parts of the judicial system.

In implementing the research suggested by our model, we have taken an eclectic approach to the study of judicial institutions, utilizing a variety of conceptual tools and methods of analysis. Where it has seemed useful we have used to analyze aspects of the courts such contrasting materials as behavioral analysis, legal materials, historical description, decisional correlations, and social background analysis. As a result we have achieved a fuller picture of the lower judiciary and its complex dimensions than a more restricted theory would have conveyed.

Given the diversity of the inputs pictured in the judicial system, we would expect decision making in the lower courts to occur in complex and varied patterns of behavior. Our findings fully support this supposition. In the district courts, for example, we found considerable differences in the decisions made in civil liberties and labor cases not only from district to district but also among judges in the same district. We found that, like other political officials, judges from different constituency backgrounds often made contrasting decisions. Indeed, in the two issue areas we investigated, there was about as much variation in behavior among district judges as may be found among judges on the Supreme Court. Appeals judges, also, differed in the direction of their decisions and in their review of the decisions of other judges and courts. In some instances, such as on the Fifth Circuit Court of Appeals, the variations in decisions on both labor and civil liberties cases were particularly noticeable.

Such patterns of decision making afford an excellent opportunity to evaluate political and legalistic theories of judicial behavior. In the chapters on decision making we accomplished an evaluation by relating decisions to some social and political characteristics. We found that factors such as partisan affiliation and social character of districts were related to the direction of decisions.

It is especially significant that decision making in the district courts evidenced considerable variation among courts, districts, and judges. Relationships and individual differences such as these are consistent with theories of political behavior and contradict legal authorities that assume monolithic behavior patterns, invariate judicial responses, and little or no relationship between decisional patterns and background factors. According to legal theories, inputs into the judicial system are screened out by the quasi-insulation of the courts and by judicial responses to legal principles and codes. On the contrary, our research indicates that social and political factors do influence judicial behavior.

A more defensible theory emphasizing legalistic factors locates such influences in the activities of elements of the legal subculture. At many points in the judicial subsystem — in judicial selection, constituency development, historical development of court organization, and in decision making — groups representing legal viewpoints intervene. The selection of judges for the lower courts provides an especially visible example of pressures by legal groups. Legal groups have also advocated the adoption of more uniform standards of law and the systematic statement of legal norms and rules as part of the decision making process. In advocating such values as legal training and judicial experiences, local bar groups, the American Bar Association Committee on the Federal Courts, and other legal spokesmen have evidenced a continual concern for legal traditions.

Equally prominent throughout our consideration of lower court politics were certain themes from the democratic subculture, for example the influence of local pressures. In the selection of lower court judges, state congressman and local elites play leading roles. The politics of judicial constituencies provide another example of the involvement of local groups, and their influence is observable throughout the history of lower court development. Decision making in the lower courts also reflects local influences, particularly in civil rights decisions in the South, where localism is especially noticeable.

Another example of democratic involvement is the impact of partisan politics. Our data indicate that parties set basic requirements for choosing lower court judges and to a large extent, preempt the process of selection. While involvement in the politics of recruitment is their most visible influence, their presence can be observed throughout the history of organizational development and also in present-day questions involving organizational and constituency development. In decision making their influence is less clear, but we did see some differences among judges with different partisan backgrounds.

Decision making in the federal judiciary, we have shown, involves interactions stemming from a variety of sources. Formally, the federal judicial process is based on relationships between the lower courts. Indeed, as Chief Justice Taft pointed out, the normal judicial process consists of an initial trial in the district court and a single appeal to the regional court. Thus, the great majority of judicial output is determined by the interactions of these two levels of courts. However, another dimension to the process is added by the interpersonal relationships among judges who establish patterns of support and conflict among themselves. Resulting behavioral patterns affect both the political direction and the substantive outcome of policies emanating from the federal courts.

Finally, our findings indicate the importance of lower court links to the Supreme Court. We contend that the Supreme Court is best conceived of as a high court, hearing personally selected cases, rather than a supreme court, which implies that the court systematically decides appeals from lower courts. The difference is significant, for the Supreme Court hears less than 10 per cent of all cases from the lower federal judiciary that are decided on appeal. The eleven appeals courts dispose of the remaining 90 per cent of the cases and do so by systematic appellate processes. In addition the appeals courts, as we have pointed out, decide important policies in their review of district court decisions.

Several additional aspects of the judicial subsystem are reflected in the Supreme Court review of lower court decisions. The importance of both judicial personalities and constituencies is indicated by the Court's greater concern with decisions from certain courts. Moreover, the Court often counters the influence of local values that are present in policies adjudicated by both district and appeals courts. A good example is the Court's review of labor cases from the Fifth Circuit and its frequent reversal of antilabor policies so often found in that circuit's decisions. In reviewing civil rights cases from Southern courts, the Court regularly reverses segregationist policies, thus nationalizing local values that were present in the lower courts as a result of judicial selection, constituency influences, and public opinion. On the other hand, the lower judiciary shape the Supreme Court in significant respects. They not only provide via initial trials the structure and content of cases placed on its agenda but also supply the substance and direction of policies to which the Court reacts in its own decisions.

Lower Court Theory

Our findings contradict important features of both the hierarchical and bureaucratic theories of the federal judiciary. Our examination of lower court politics enables us to identify specific inadequacies in the theoretical assumptions made by each. For example, our investigations show that a key assumption of the hierarchical idea — that politically significant activities do not occur in the lower courts but are identified only in the Supreme Court — is mistaken. On the contrary, it is clear that many important issues are settled in the district and appeals courts. Moreover, evidence in Chapters Six and Seven shows no rigorously structured flow of cases from lower to higher courts, as the hierarchical theory would predict. Instead, the passage of cases from one level of court to another on appeal is dependent on a number of diverse factors and corresponds to no neat diagram of legal authority. Moreover, interactions in the judiciary do not follow stipulated patterns of authority but embody considerable variation of conflict and agreement among different courts and judges. Neither the appeals courts nor the Supreme Court review lower court decisions in consistent political directions, as might be implied from an authoritarian ordering of lower and higher courts. Indeed, the Supreme Court will sometimes support district courts over appeals courts in particular decisions even when an appeals court has reversed a district court.

We observed further evidence casting doubt on the hierarchical interpretation in the recruitment of lower court personnel and in the structure of lower court constituencies. In practice the Supreme Court has rarely intervened in judicial selection in the lower courts or exercised political control over proceedings in the districts or circuits. One purpose of the creation of the Judicial Conference and the judicial councils was to provide the means for more systematic direction of the federal courts. There is no evidence, however, that these meetings have brought much hierarchical direction to the courts or that they have weakened the district and regional constituencies. Both district and appeals courts continue to embody substantial degrees of local control made possible by the relative independence of the judicial constituencies in the lower courts and by local control over such matters as court staffing and many judicial procedures. The absence of hierarchical control in the lower courts is further documented in the history of lower court organization, where there is considerable emphasis on localism in the judiciary but little mention of issues looking toward more central control of the courts. Although there has been some progress in maintaining standards of uniformity by means of legal codes, these aspects of the legal culture have provided little means of enforcement by centralized direction.

Our findings also do not support the bureaucratic interpretation of the federal judiciary, a theory which considers the lower courts the bottom echelons of an organization responding to the directives of the Supreme Court. For example, the bureaucratic theory assumes that there should be considerable in-service promotion, or movement of personnel from one level of court to another, particularly in response to pressures from the Supreme Court. Yet, the Supreme Court not only plays no active part in lower court recruitment, but there is also comparatively little elevation of district court judges to the appeals courts. Rather, decisions on recruitment for each level of the courts respond to somewhat different pressures and involve different political actors. Chapters Five and Six indicate that decision making, while reflecting political cues from the top of the court system, is also influenced significantly by the environmental character of different courts. The entire history of lower court development with respect to such features as organization and staffing has not been primarily concerned with such bureaucratic issues as administrative centralization and efficiency and management, but has emphasized policies concerning the separate political roles of the different courts. The creation of the appeals courts and the definition of district court functions, for example, were in response not so much to administrative needs as to political pressure.

On the other hand, our study corroborates two theoretical perspectives suggested for the lower courts. One of these, Peltason's pathbreaking *Federal Courts in the Political Process,* described federal judges "as participants in the political process" and their activities as "determined by and . . . not above the group struggle." [1] Peltason's emphasis on politics as group activity reflects an earlier, now old-fashioned, concern with the seminal work of Arthur Bentley. Our investigation of the judicial process indicates that judges are responsive to a wide range of influences, not just groups and interests. But our study indicates Peltason was surely right when he placed courts as participants in a dynamic political process in which every action and interaction involved patterns of political behavior.

The results of our investigation are in closest agreement with Dolbeare's recent theory of the courts as involved in "continuing local political processes." [2] According to Dolbeare each judicial process proceeds according to "distinctive regional and local political-culture based approaches" and judges serve as "mediators between the judicial and local political subsystems." His theory also emphasizes, as we have throughout this work, the interactions between democratic and legal subcultures. It brings out the importance of local and regional political factors in such aspects of the judiciary as recruitment of court personnel, judicial constituencies, and decision making in lower courts. Finally, his perspective provides a model broad enough to encompass the various influences that we have identified in the activities of the lower courts.

Lower Court Research

To implement our theoretical conceptions we have utilized a variety of materials on lower court activities. The collection and processing of these materials has provided us with useful information on a variety of data problems encountered in researching district and appeals courts. Our experience enables us to comment specifically

[1] J. W. Peltason, *Federal Courts in the Political Process* (New York: Doubleday, 1955), p. 4.

[2] Kenneth M. Dolbeare, "The Federal District Courts and Urban Public Policy: An Exploratory Study (1960–1967)" in Joel Grossman and Joseph Tanenhaus, eds., *Frontiers of Judicial Research* (New York: John Wiley, 1968), p. 391.

on some of the problems discussed in Chapter One concerning difficulties in obtaining data for lower court analysis.

In general our research methods have been flexible, and we have
utilized many kinds of institutional data including behavioral, decisional, and legal data. Typically, chapters have been based on such
different kinds of data as court decisions, social background characteristics of judges, constituency features, and historical information.
Our experience confirms Peltason's observation that judicial institutions, like other political institutions, can be usefully investigated
by many different kinds of empirical data. While there are distinctive features of judicial institutions, namely the elements of the legal
subculture, we have investigated these factors along with the nonlegal aspects of the judiciary. For example, we have looked at the
influence of legal pressures, groups, and codes at the same time that
we have examined voting patterns, partisan influences, and constituency effects.

Our research in Chapters Five and Six employed lower court decisions. These data require special handling because of their legalistic
character, the large number of cases involved, and the absence of
clear categorical divisions. However, we were able to use lower
court opinions to investigate decision making in a large number of
courts and to focus on a number of important behavioral problems.
Our experience indicates no difficulty either in obtaining such data,
in coding it for political analysis, or in utilizing the data for political
science. While whole populations of decisions can rarely be used, as
in the study of the Supreme Court, accurate and reliable data can
be obtained through the use of sampling and stratification methods.
Finally, we may conclude that the great number of lower courts,
their widespread and heterogeneous character, and the different
levels of court organization present an important opportunity for
research and analysis. Precisely because of the great diversity in
environments, judges, and decisions, there are resources for examining a variety of judicial problems. For that reason the lower courts
embody more opportunities for the analysis of a greater variety of
behavioral and decisional problems than does the Supreme Court.
Convincing proof exists in the work of such authors as Peltason,
Dolbeare, and Goldman who have explored certain aspects of lower
court politics through the use of empirical data.

Proposals for Reform

Our investigation has spotlighted a number of quite controversial political outcomes concerning not only specific decisions but arguments over the manner in which the courts should be staffed, their constituencies set, and their decisions reviewed among levels of courts. Some of these outcomes have been quite visible to various political publics and have generated a number of responses in the form of policy proposals or "judicial reforms." These proposals for change let us know which lower court activities are most visible and also identify those elements in the legal and democratic subcultures that are most interested in particular activities.

One of the most persistent suggestions made in the Congress for change in the lower courts concerns judicial tenure. Typical proposals would modify the life tenure presently enjoyed by establishing limited terms of office with provision for a re-appointment or, alternatively, provide for regular elections after initial appointment. Such proposals would certainly make both district and circuit judges more responsive to regional and local constituency pressures in decision making. Life tenure and the virtual absence of harrassment by political impeachment procedures have enabled individual judges such as district judges Wright from Louisiana and Johnson from Alabama to follow patterns of decision making that are "independent" of constituencies. While most judges are influenced, as we have shown, by their constituency environments and reflect local values and public opinion, others follow national standards in decision making. Ever since the Jacksonian movement affected state judicial politics in important ways, democratic groups have been interested in linking judicial behavior more strongly to local politics through such means as popular elections and nominations. Not yet, however, have suggestions for more local responsiveness induced significant changes in judicial tenure.

Another proposed reform, the rotation of judges, is related to the influence of democratic values on lower courts in quite a different way. While judges normally rotate in the circuits and districts to fill in for absent judges or to help out with overloaded dockets, they do so relatively infrequently and unsystematically. Usually, judges hold court and conduct judicial affairs in the local or regional constituency boundaries within which they are appointed. Our study included only a single case, that of Judge Davies in the district court of Arkansas, in which a rotated judge from an outside district participated in an important decision. Suggestions for judicial rotation usually emanate within judicial council meetings or are suggested by legal interests. Considering the importance of lower court associations with local constituencies, democratic interests are unlikely to accede to requests for rotation procedures that would mitigate the influence of local values.

The pressure to maximize pretrial procedures in the lower courts is an outgrowth of the search for more efficient ways to handle backlogs of cases. Although the Judicial Conference has frequently suggested the use of more pretrials in decision making and has sponsored seminars and instructional sessions, pretrials are used, as we have indicated, only sporadically. They vary from court to court both in frequency and the manner in which they are used. Here again the independence of district courts from any real central supervision is reflected in the variable behavior of different judges.

In those courts that do use pretrials we find evidence that such procedures affect decision making in important ways. Their most important effect is to materially reduce, or in some cases, to eliminate litigation and the attendant legal procedures that embody important traditions of the legal subculture. In so doing the judge is more clearly an individual decision maker not circumscribed by his environment of legal procedures. While individual judges do lay down rules for the procedures used in pretrials, these are individually constructed on an *ad hoc* basis and embody the judge's values rather than reflect legal traditions. Yet there is also less opportunity for the representation of democratic pressures through their intrusion in litigation. Exactly what effects pretrials will have on decision making is a matter of speculation, for few empirical studies have been conducted.

Modification of the selection system is a perennial reform suggested for the federal courts. Legal interests have long advocated greater participation by the bar and other legal groups. The inclusion in 1954 of the Committee on the Federal Judiciary of the

American Bar Association in the selection process is a concrete instance of the participation of legal interests through the recommendations and ratings made by this committee. Experience has indicated, however, that this committee affects judicial selection only peripherally; only in setting minimum standards and deciding marginal cases has the influence of the committee been decisive. Selection of lower court judges remains firmly in the hands of the state Senators and the local parties, while it is the function of legal groups and the American Bar Association committee to set certain minimum legal standards, the most important of which is the inclusion of minimum legal training.

In the overall proposals for judicial reform, the tension between democratic and legal interests is clear. Both aspire to affect changes in judicial selection — democratic interests through the advocacy of limited terms and possible election of judges, legal interests by proposals to increase legal training standards and through the intervention of the Committee on the Federal Judiciary. Both also would affect the decisional process by indirect means. Rotational schemes and pretrials, proposed by legal advocates, have implications for decision making but so do suggestions concerning restricted tenure of judges, advocated by democratic interests. Thus far the American Bar Association has managed but slight improvements in their influence on judicial selection. Pretrial procedures continue to exercise steady but comparatively slight influences on decision making. Otherwise, there have been few modifications of judicial structures and procedures in the lower federal judiciary nor do any seem likely in the near future.

The Federal Courts: Synthesis of Two Cultures

The lower federal courts are unique in the American federal system in the way in which they diffuse national power. Of all the federal political systems, very few — for example the United States and Argentina — locate the national judiciary throughout the states. As a result, lower court decision makers are the most important national officials who are systematically localized in the performance of their functions. The result of such organization is a diffusion of national values, tempered by local political considerations and behaviors.

Our study has shown that in the performance of their role, the courts combine the features of both the legal and democratic subcultures, responding to the demands of both in a continuing dialectic of political conflict. Although the federal courts remain the great repository for the legal subculture of American society, they also respond sensitively to the values of democratic society. Their very location and isolation in district constituencies and regional appellate institutions place them close to the people. Moreover, the selection of judges in both the district and regional courts takes place by processes which primarily involve local values and the influence of local politicians. In addition, the lack of central direction over lower federal court decision making permits great variety in judicial behavior, and this too is an important step in the direction of popular responsibility. In fact, the opinions accompanying controversial decisions in particular courts sometimes read like reports to constituencies.

These responses to the norms of democracy suggest the answer to the question, posed earlier in our study: How have the federal courts remained intact from the ravages of popular change? Their lack of change is only apparent. In fact, they have demonstrated great response to the changing tides of political parties and the parochial power of state decision makers. Although the advocates of the legal order have found the inroads made by the political forces distasteful, they have not succeeded in substantially reducing the political influences over judicial selection nor in standardizing decision making in the relatively isolated structures of local judicial constituencies. Thus, though the federal courts represent the very embodiment of legal order, they also represent institutions intrinsically linked to popular democracy.

The fusion in the judicial system between the demands of legal and democratic subcultures is perhaps nowhere better seen than in the areas of "judicial independence" and "uniform standards of law." A primary value of the legal order has been the independence of the decision maker. Stress has been placed on judges' detachment from overt links with popular institutions, the insulation of the courts from expressions of popular opinions, and the safety of the judges from the vicissitudes of popular change. Life tenure, indirect selection, and restricted access have institutionalized this value. Yet, court decision makers are chosen by partisans, they have usually been involved in political activity, they are residents of local communities, and they continue to live and adjudicate claims in a local political milieu. Hence, one may ask of "judicial independence," independence from what? Certainly judicial independence in America does not mean an objective, nor detached, judiciary. Rather, it broadens the range of possible political responses that a judge may make. A district judge may thus respond to community or local values, or he may espouse other group values held outside the community.

If judicial independence is not achieved, neither is the objective of a predictable, coordinated, national standard of law. Our study has confirmed Jack Peltason's suggestion that the lower federal courts are important decision makers with much opportunity for independence and differences. The appellate process, by which uniformity of law is mainly achieved, is largely performed by the eleven courts of appeals. Only in a small portion of cases does the Supreme Court undertake an appellate review, and this fact has led us to conclude that the Supreme Court is not primarily an appellate court. In addition, the district courts deal not only with important public issues, but in a large portion of their cases they have the final word on the direction of public policy. Thus, although directions do often come from the Supreme Court, and although some aspects of hierarchy of court structure do exist, integrated and coordinated national law does not emerge from the federal judicial system. Not only can the Supreme Court not adequately supervise the decisions and personnel of the lower federal courts, but the judicial council movement, which seeks integration of judicial activities, has neither the power nor the resources to perform this function. In many instances, local views of national laws prevail through decisions of district courts supported by regional courts. National values, filtered through local judges, become modified or ignored, and national law becomes shaded by a variety of local behaviors and decisions.

The advocates of the legal order, however, continue in their efforts to maximize control over the courts and institutionalize legal values in the federal judiciary. Their control over the socialization and training of legal professionals, the efforts of the American Bar Association to intrude into the recruitment process, and the creation of the judicial councils and conferences are all instances of influence over the federal courts. The adoption of codes and other efforts to systematize legal values and procedures indicate limited victories for the advocates of the legal order over the diversity of local practices in federal jurisprudence.

As political institutions, the lower federal courts face many of the same problems as other political agencies. Their constituency structure, clearly designed in some respects to provide representative judicial institutions for political clienteles, face some problems of malapportionment. Although judicial malapportionment is barely discernable as a political issue, we have suggested that it poses important problems for the operation of the judiciary. The recruitment of judges continues to excite controversy, just as recruitment for other political institutions does. The familiar charges of inadequate qualifications, patronage, and partisan favoritism, so often heard in the bureaucracy, are transferred to the lower courts. Coordinating actions into uniform policies, a problem common to the executive department, plagues the courts as well. And the tensions between national and state decision makers in the federal system are manifested often in judicial conflicts.

If the conflict and synthesis of the legal and democratic subcultures were one object of our study, an emphasis on the federal judiciary as a system was another. We have suggested that segmented views of the system become easily distorted and that emphasis on Supreme Court behavior without the investigation of the lower courts neglects important features of the federal judicial process. A distinctive aspect of the federal judiciary is the making of decisions by interaction among court institutions. Though district and appellate courts make sufficient unreviewed policy decisions to maintain an institutional separateness and identity, many important policies are screened and processed through a system of interactions. To a large extent, this interaction reduces the local character of federal courts. It is, therefore, more than a set of procedures; it is an enlarging, transforming process by which individual judges and their policies are supported or rebuffed by individuals and blocs of judicial superiors. Decision making in the federal courts takes place on two levels. One part is concluded within constituencies, is largely unsupervised, and arouses little reaction. Another part, involving visible and important policies, is done after a series of interactions and responses within the system. In the latter case, both intracourt and intercourt behaviors constitute important ingredients of the decision making process. By investigating the federal courts as a system within a system, we have sought to emphasize and understand both the political consequences of their activities and the political forces that shape their behavior.

The politics of federal courts embody many judicial institutions, behaviors, and policies. Numerous as the various interactions of participants and courts may seem, the judiciary does "articulate as a system." Just as in the Supreme Court, there is order, regularity, predictable interaction, and discoverable relationships. The lower courts' more complex behaviors and institutions, though reflected in a different order of data from that available for the Supreme Court, present exciting opportunities for making generalizations about the operation of the lower federal courts. The model we have suggested in Chapter One describes a framework for analysis of the federal judiciary, and the succeeding chapters have examined certain features of its operation.

Although the dialectic of legal and democratic cultures has created many of the problems and conflicts of the lower courts, it also appears to have built a system presenting the benefits of both. The distinctive idea of the federal court system — a diffusion of national power throughout the states by means of judicial institutions — has added an important political agency to American democracy. It has not only provided a channel for legal and national values but has done so in institutions and practices which support America's democratic culture. Thus, the "remote and removed" institutions of government contemplated by Madison have been modified and fitted to the growing democratic expectations of a changing political system.